HOW TO PLAY
PAR
FIVES

Peter Smith

Colour Library Books

CLB 3432
Published in 1994 by Colour Library Books
© 1993 Colour Library Books Ltd, Godalming, Surrey
All rights reserved
Printed and bound in Singapore by Kim Hup Lee Printing Co. Pte. Ltd.
ISBN 1-85833-059-9

Contents

Peter Smith

The author Peter Smith has worked as a writer and marketing consultant for over twenty-five years. He has published books on travel, classical composers and the painter Constable. Peter also paints, primarily in oils.

Widely travelled, he has worked as a journalist in the aviation and travel industries, and was the editor of travel magazines in London and New York. Peter lives in Madrid, Spain.

Introduction

To the average player a par-5 can be intimidating, stretching out 500 yards or so into the distance, tempting us to hit the ball farther than we ever have before.

To the professional on the other hand, a par-5 is a birdie opportunity – two good shots and he will be safely on green.

But playing par-5s wisely and well is in reality not so difficult for the average golfer like you and me. As more than one professional in the book points out, playing a par-5 is no more demanding than hitting three middle irons about 160 yards each – something that most of us are quite capable of. Using the stroke index, rather than gazing hopefully into the distance, can give many of us another shot to use. Learning to play the hole strategically, giving ourselves an easy next 'move', is another important secret for success.

As the professionals show us within these pages, perhaps the key to playing winning golf on par-5s is to know your game and to plan – and not to 'hit and hope'.

Kennemer, Holland
Jim Buchanan, Club Professional

2nd hole, 563 yards

Jim Buchanan started his professional career at Turnberry, the world-famous Scottish course that has produced so many great teaching professionals.

He is now club professional at Kennemer Golf Club on the shore of the North Sea in Holland. Kennemer is a championship course which regularly hosts the KLM Dutch Open. It is a typical links course with rolling fairways and scrubby vegetation, and with bushes rather than the towering trees typical of inland courses.

Sea mist is a hazard on this course at certain times of the year and on the cold October afternoon Jim and I headed out onto the course, the mist was rolling in fast and hastening the early dusk.

The course itself is a composite of three 9-hole courses, giving a good variety of holes to play for the members, although the eighteen championship holes do not vary. The hole that we played was the 563-yard 2nd, a difficult par-5 with a stroke index of 3, so its challenge can easily be gauged.

Kennemer

- **Damp weather, rain and mist hold the ball back a little, so compensate for this**
- **Don't swing faster into the wind**
- **With a following wind tee the ball slightly higher**
- **With the wind against, tee the ball lower and move the body over the ball earlier**

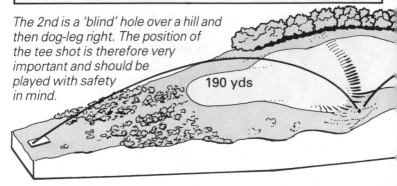

The 2nd is a 'blind' hole over a hill and then dog-leg right. The position of the tee shot is therefore very important and should be played with safety in mind.

190 yds

The Club Professional at Kennemer is Scotsman Jim Buchanan, whose career began at Turnberry.

The members' tee makes it a more modest 520 yards, with an initial carry across bushes (out of which it would be impossible to play if you completely duff the tee-shot) to a hilly ridge which blocks out the distant green. After the ridge the hole dog-legs right and then runs downhill to a very tight approach, just 10 yards wide.

"It's impossible to reach the green in two," Jim told me as we stood on the tee. "The top of the hill is about 190 yards away, and is also the widest part of the fairway, though only about 30 yards across. You must stay right because the ground slopes quite a bit from right to left; any ball going left is likely to end up being completely unplayable.

"Play a 3-wood off the tee, aiming slightly to the right of the

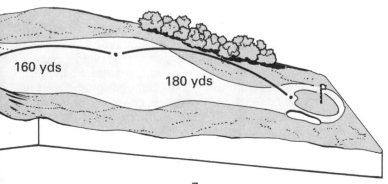

160 yds

180 yds

Always take the time to properly survey your tee-shot. Absorb all the information that you need to determine the best aiming position. Here the arrow points to the wise choice. To be left would definitely be too dangerous. To the right on the other hand is fairly safe.

top of the hill. That is a flat, safe area for the second shot.''

The wind was slightly behind us, coming from left to right so Jim recommended teeing the ball slightly higher than usual, to take advantage of it.

''It will hold the ball up more and, once up there, will take it further. Conversely, when the wind is against you, keep it low, by teeing lower and moving the body over the ball earlier.

''When you are on the fairway with an iron you need to have the ball further back in your stance with the club face slightly hooded (not closed!) and the hands ahead of the ball. Then use the lower part of the body to 'drive' the shot, turning the right knee in earlier, pulling the upper body through the ball with more power. What you don't want to do is to swing faster – that won't give the average player distance into the wind.

''Into the wind you are always moving ahead of the ball.''

He also suggested teeing the ball slightly higher if you are short, and a little lower if you are tall, because the angle of the swing-plane is different. The variation in the swing-plane between, say, Sandy Lyle and Ian Woosnam, is evident when you watch them play.

The first shot, using the 3-wood, was aimed slightly too far

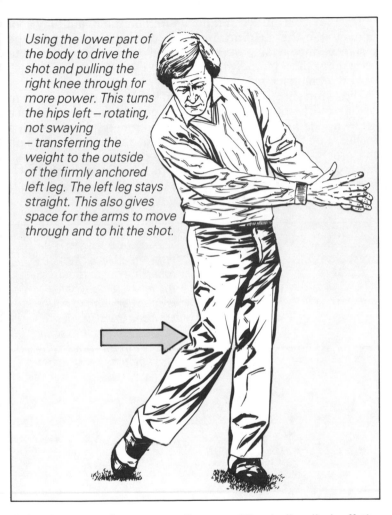

Using the lower part of the body to drive the shot and pulling the right knee through for more power. This turns the hips left – rotating, not swaying – transferring the weight to the outside of the firmly anchored left leg. The left leg stays straight. This also gives space for the arms to move through and to hit the shot.

right, but was the correct distance. The ball rolled off the fairway and ended up in some very fluffy rough with an excellent lie, enabling me to get a 5-iron to it easily.

Having walked out onto the middle of the fairway to survey the scene, choosing the point that would give me the best possible shot next time, I aimed at that point. The ball landed almost exactly where I wanted it although slightly short of the 150 metre post (what a help these markers are). The choice then is either a long iron or fairway wood to the green (I had about 180 yards to go) or a short iron to lay up for a pitch in. You need to bear in mind that the approach is very narrow indeed, just eleven yards across, with a bunker front right.

That day I was lucky, hitting a 4-iron off the beautifully kept fairway into the swirling mist. The direction was right – the distance, once again, was very slightly short. You do have to remember that damp weather, when the air is 'heavier', will hold the ball back a bit.

The 4-iron shot landed two feet off the green, directly in front of the pin a tempting ten feet away. A gentle 9-iron with the face really hooded just clipped the ball and rolled it to about nine inches from the hole. Taking the flag out and laying it down off the green, I wished I had a playing partner who would tell me it was a 'gimme'. It's so easy to miss these, isn't it? A gentle tap on the flat surface and it rolled those few difficult inches to the cup – and dropped in! A five!

The follow through. The right knee has kicked round almost to touch the firm left leg. There is space enough to hit the shot and the shoulders are pulled round to the 'square' follow through position. Note that the finish is here perfectly balanced.

Lake Nona, Florida, USA
Gregor Jamieson, Club Professional

15th hole, 578 yards

A few miles from Orlando, set in beautiful woodland inters-persed with lakes, is the exclusive residential and golf complex of Lake Nona. The golf course, formally opened in November 1988, is already ranked well inside the top 100 in the world by a highly respected golf publication.

Gregor Jamieson, son of the highly admired Bob Jamieson of Turnberry fame, is the golf professional here. The member-ship of the club is by invitation only, which gives some indication of its exclusivity. The club is also the base for the world-famous coach David Leadbetter. On the day of my visit Mrs Leadbetter was busy giving a lesson to several of the lady members, prior to a tournament.

Gregor chose the difficult 15th hole for our lesson, a very long 578-yard par-5 with a stroke index of two – only the 543-yard 2nd is rated more difficult. To be confronted, standing on the elevated tee, with this big distance is challenging.

To the left of the fairway hole is the lake, guarded by trees for the first 100 yards, then by a huge flat bunker which runs an incredible 240 yards alongside the fairway. If you ever land in it, then just lob out sideways!

The fairway itself, particularly on the right, is undulating, so

Gregor Jamieson (right) is Lake Nona's Club Professional. On the left is world famous teacher David Leadbetter.

On the left is the enormous 240-yard long bunker. The bunker separates the rolling fairway from the large lake which dominates the 15th hole.

the ball will normally roll down into one of the many hollows or slightly left, which is the place to be for the second shot.

"The first thing to do is ignore the driver," Gregor told me. "It's a club the higher handicapper could well do without."

Several studies have been made in the United States for the 12–20 handicapper. Almost all of them show that golfers hitting a 3-wood off the tee will achieve greater distance (carry and roll) than those using the driver. An average player can achieve 200 yards with a 3-wood, though he would achieve

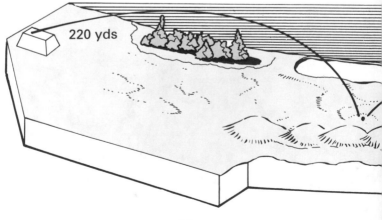

220 yds

slightly less off a fairway.

"This hole then becomes two 3-woods and a 160-yard long iron to the green – or a 5- or 7-wood," Gregor continued.

Measuring that way, where you cut the yardage into achievable distances, takes some of the fear out of the hole.

"Having taken the 3-wood out of the bag the next thing is to focus on a specific target at which to aim.

"Not just the middle of the fairway, but a definite, definable target like the branch on the tree slightly right."

The tree itself was way out of range but using it as a 'direction-finder' helps concentrate your mind on where you are aiming to go. Invariably you will hit close to the target if it is easy to define.

"You must be focused," said Gregor.

The best shot here was to aim slightly right, at that target, with a small amount of hook, bringing the ball round right to left. The ball does travel further this way.

"Going back many years Scots greenkeepers always used to mow the fairways in a clockwise motion, from the tee out," Gregor told me, "so the grain on the left would be towards the hole whilst that on the right would be back towards the tee. Thus a ball in the left side of the fairway would have a much

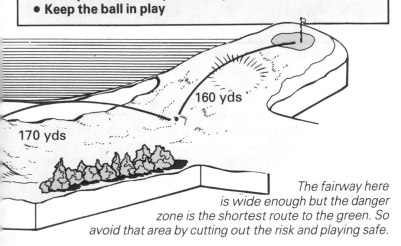

Lake Nona

- Unless you are comfortable off the tee with a driver, use a 3-wood
- Cut the yardage of a hole into achievable distances
- Always focus on a specific target
- Keep the ball in play

160 yds

170 yds

The fairway here is wide enough but the danger zone is the shortest route to the green. So avoid that area by cutting out the risk and playing safe.

If you choose a specific landmark on which to focus your concentration (for example a branch on a distant tree), you will find that your accuracy will improve.

better lie. Although that doesn't happen much in America, there are still a few places in Scotland where the habit exists."

With the roll on the tee-shot the ball ended up about 220 yards off the tee, with about 330 to go.

"The thing to do now is to knock it forward, in play, getting as much distance as you can but keeping it *in play!*"

The approach shot was another opportunity for Gregor to demonstrate the importance of having a specific target to aim at. He walked forward to the green to demonstrate where the player from 100 yards or so should be aiming, pointing to the flag and suggesting that he should aim about two feet up the pin.

Obviously for a chip shot, where the ball will run, that is not relevant because the chip shot is more like a putt in its ground/air time ratios.

"For a pitch in, though, you must have a specific target."

As the day was warm we also discussed the effect of heat on a golf ball.

"In hot weather it is much easier to compress the ball – just like a squash ball performing better when it's hot – so it will travel further. You can also use a higher compression ball (100) when it's warm. Conversely, when it's cold use a lower compression, even down to a ladies ball which is 85 compression. Humidity, too, decreases the ball's carrying capacity so a lower compression is better in wet conditions, either humidity or rain.

"The main point to remember though," Gregor told me as we headed back to the pro shop and the splendid clubhouse, "is to be focused!"

To get close to the pin with an approach shot from up to 100 yards out, aim about two feet up the pin as a focal point, as Gregor Jamieson demonstrates. This helps concentration and precision.

3

Bokskogens, Sweden
Janne Larsson, Club Professional

5th hole, 552 yards

"Playing a par-5 is simple – all you need to be able to do is to putt from two feet!"

Yes, I know what you are thinking – it brought a smile to my face too, when Janne Larsson, the professional at Bokskogens Golf Club, just south of Malmo in Sweden, told me this one cold December afternoon. We were sitting by the log fire in his stone cottage next to the clubhouse. As a gentle rain fell outside he explained that it was not quite that simple, but the philosophy is right.

"To play good golf you need to be confident in your ability to successfully play the shot facing you. Thus the most important shot on a par-5 is *the final putt* – the one from a couple of feet that will make the ball drop in the hole – that's the only time you score.

"Be confident in that putt, and the long approach putt from the edge of the green becomes easier. From 30 feet you don't

---

Bokskogens

- **The final putt is the only time you score**
- **Plan the hole the way you want to play it; don't let it dictate to you**
- **Putt comfortably from two feet and you will putt more confidently from 30 feet**
- **You must practise to improve, but don't aim too high too quickly**

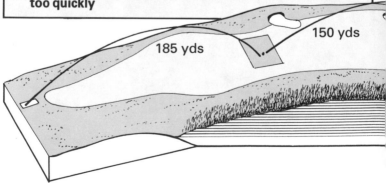

150 yds

185 yds

'All you need to do to play a par-5 well is to be able to putt from two feet!' claims Janne Larsson.

expect to get the ball in the hole; what you want to do is put it within a two-feet circle of the pin. Confidence in that two-footer gives you the confidence to putt from 30 feet.

"And if you are confident putting to two feet from 30 feet you know that once the ball is on the green you are down in two, so the pitch shot from 65 yards is really much simpler.

"Confidence in your ability to pitch from 65 yards means your long iron shot, to anywhere around 65 yards short – or a hundred – will get you down in three.

"Confidence in your ability to hit a long iron to 65 yards or 100 yards short of the green makes the drive much simpler, because you know all you have to do is to hit to a point from which you can hit a long iron safely."

Janne has this wonderful talent for making golf sound such a

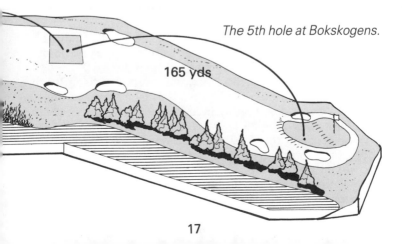

The 5th hole at Bokskogens.

165 yds

A shorter tee shot keeps the second shot out of danger but gives enough distance for the third shot to get to the green.

simple game. I asked if I could have a hot-line to him from a mobile phone out on the golf course!

"Analyse your game," he advised. "Learn where you are going wrong – make a note of the shots you are missing, or not hitting as well as you would like, and then work on correcting them.

"Everyone has a certain handicap. Why? It's because they are not as expert as they might be, or might like to be, on certain shots. Work backwards from the pin, from that last putt from a couple of feet. Once you have got that right, move back to the front of the green and hit long putts until you can get every one within two feet.

"Then work on the approach shots, pitching or chipping from any distance you like until you can hit the green from anywhere with every shot. Once that is perfect move back to the long iron, then the drive. Far too many people play golf the wrong way round, trying to get the drive right first and forgetting the scoring shots. *You only score with the last shot!*

"Of course you need to realise what you want to play golf for – do you want to improve or are you quite happy just going out hitting a few balls and enjoying the 19th hole?

"If you want to improve, then you must practise. But don't aim too high too quickly. There's no instant way to improve, you need to work and work if you want to knock five shots off your handicap."

We discussed the value of keeping a close record of your shots on each round of golf, and of analysing the areas where you are dropping shots.

"The other vital aspect of golf for handicap players is to *use the stroke index on the hole you are playing*," continued Janne.

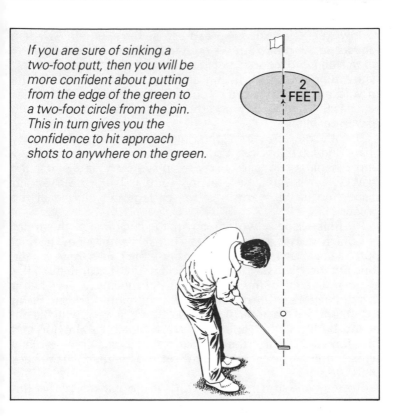

If you are sure of sinking a two-foot putt, then you will be more confident about putting from the edge of the green to a two-foot circle from the pin. This in turn gives you the confidence to hit approach shots to anywhere on the green.

"Course designers know how difficult each hole is – if the index gives you a stroke, use it! Thus, a super-difficult par-5 is, for most players, a fairly easy par-6. Even 540 yards can be reached in four – just 135 yards each shot! Imagine the par 5 is a series of easy par-3s, each of about 160 yards. Plant a flag, in your mind, every 160 yards and hit to it. That way you could reach a 650-yard hole in four – surely that's no problem? Most par-5s are only around 550 yards, or less."

Talking to someone as experienced and friendly as Janne really inspires self-confidence; it makes you wonder why some people try to tell you that golf is so difficult. Here is a man who, over years of teaching, has learnt the essence of golf and is now happy to pass on that important lesson. Just listening to him makes you feel that, if only you could have him by you on every shot, gving you confidence, making you *think*, you could play better than your handicap on every round. If we amateur players, you and I, could remember the things that Janne and other professionals tell us, we really could beat our handicap on every round.

However, as darkness spread across the southern Swedish landscape, we made our way out to the most interesting par-5 on this beautiful course, set in a forest of pine, beech and oak, with a huge lake which, in July and August, is home to 150 pairs of wild geese – with their young the lake's colony of geese reaches 800 before they start their September migration south to warmer climes.

The 5th hole, 552 yards long, runs alongside the lake, a fairly sharp dog-leg right close to the green. It is a true par-5, virtually unreachable in two for even the top players who take part in the PLM Swedish Open here every August. True to our earlier discussion in the warmth of the cottage, we started at the green.

The green itself is two-tiered with the flag often on the upper tier which is small and guarded by bunkers either side. The final putt needs to be from this upper tier if the flag is there, so the long putt needs to be hit with sufficient force to climb the hill.

The front edge of the green is narrow and always wet, being in a slight hollow. The approach shot, therefore, needs to be hit to the centre of the green if possible. Some players, with the pin at the back on the upper tier, are tempted to aim for that position but, because the only safe shot in is a draw, the ball would continue bouncing and roll on into the rough at the back of the green.

The only safe shot into the green is to aim either slightly right or for the centre of the green; most players will be hitting from the dog-leg, about 150 yards from the pin, a shot that is easily reachable with a middle or short iron.

The shot to this dog-leg will be from the tee-shot landing area, about 180 yards off the normal yellow tee (which makes the hole 493 yards – some 60 yards short of the championship tee). The tee-shot, therefore, needs to be only about 185 yards, the second a short lay-up of 145 yards, the third a 160-yard approach, although if the second shot is hit past the dog-leg staying left, the approach is that much shorter. The illustration of the hole shows how to plan the approach, and this is the key. Plan the hole the way *you* want to play it – dictate to the course, don't let it dictate to you!

The three shots to the green, therefore, are, in order from the tee: 185 yards, 145 and 160. A slightly longer second shot (though the shorter lay-up is better), would pass the hazards and leave you a third shot of about 140 yards, an easily controllable shot, providing you are confident on this shot, as well as the long putt, and the short putt!

Building it from the pin back certainly takes on an entirely new meaning, thanks to Janne Larsson.

Rungsted, Denmark
Bob Beattie, Club Professional

18th hole, 482 yards

"How," I asked Bob Beattie, professional at Rungsted, Denmark's premier golf course, as we stood on the 18th tee with 482 yards of fairway stretching out in front of us, "do you get that extra 30 yards or so out of a drive?"

With a long fairway dotted with hazards an extra 30 yards would make the approach shot to the green so much easier. It is something that we all dream of, isn't it? Hitting one straight down the middle well over 200 yards!

The reply startled me a little but having given it some thought I now understand.

"Why do you want to hit a ball straight? The top pros don't!

"Even Jack Nicklaus admits that he, and his fellow tour professionals, can only hit about forty per cent of their shots straight. Do you think you can improve on that?

"And you ask for an extra ten per cent on distance – have you tried asking your garage to make your car go ten per cent faster? If they did, it would take more than ten per cent extra engine power."

Bob explained, "Very few top players hit a ball straight. For a start golf courses are not built straight. They also have hazards along the fairway which you have to work the ball round. Whenever you get on a golf course you need to be able to analyse what shape of shot you need to avoid dangers and then to produce it.

'Why hit a ball straight?' asks Bob Beattie, Club Professional at Rungsted. 'The pros don't!'

"Secondly a ball with draw, moving right to left, will travel further than one hit dead straight. So for extra distance learn to draw the ball slightly. A ball hit with fade loses about ten per cent on distance to one hit dead straight – one with draw adds about five per cent.

"I can understand you wanting to hit the ball to the middle of the fairway but that doesn't mean hitting it straight. Sometimes you might need to fade it, sometimes to hit it very high to clear some trees, or sometimes keep it low – in the wind for example.

"A wonderful way to practise is to see how you can work the ball. Go out on the practice area or a driving range and, once you have warmed up, hit four balls to a specific, marked area, using any club you like. Hit a draw, a fade, a high shot and a low shot; all of them must land in the same area. Hitting fifty 6-irons all the same shape might help you hit 6-irons, but learning how to work the ball will be far more beneficial."

I had never heard such advice before, yet it makes so much sense, for how often do you find golf courses that require a fade on every shot – or a draw? This exercise now forms a major part of my practice routine, however short or long. At the driving range I now go through the bag trying to hit four shots to the same spot – fade, draw, high, low. Try it! Your golf will improve, I promise.

"And as for extra distance," continued Bob, "that only comes

Rungsted

- **Analyse dangers carefully and decide how to avoid them**
- **A ball hit with draw travels further than one hit dead straight**
- **Practise working the ball with fade, with draw, high and low**
- **For extra distance accelerate into the ball but maintain control at all times**

210 yds

from swinging faster. The clubhead speed at the moment of contact is all that matters. Yet everybody has their own maximum swing speed – big guys like Lyle and Faldo can generate more power because they hit the ball faster. Practise improving your swing speed to *your* maximum, but maintain control of the ball. Extra distance is pointless if the ball is out-of-bounds. The only 'instant' way to add extra distance is to buy graphite shafted clubs. They do add 15 to 20 yards to your shots."

Rungsted is the course that hosts the Danish Open as well as several WPGA Tour events. The first shot from the 8th tee needs to be hit left with fade, staying away from the out-of-bounds down the right and a bunker strategically placed to catch a short drive. The bunker on the right is at 165 yards; the one on the left, where the fairway slopes left to right, is even trickier at 190 yards.

Hence the shaped shot, aimed at the left bunker with fade, should come round into the centre of the fairway – straight down the middle without being straight!

"We now come to the easiest shot in golf," Bob told me. "The second shot on a par-5 when you have no chance of reaching the green is easy because there is no pressure. All you need to do is to hit it down the fairway, with as much distance as you can. Yet if you don't achieve too much distance your next shot is still going to reach the green – unless you completely top it or miss it altogether!"

From the bunker on the left you have 255 yards to go, with a narrow entrance caused by trees and a bunker at 106 yards from the front of the green. A shot, therefore, of 148 yards could get you into trouble, but not too much.

If you have learnt how to work the ball, you can aim left with fade from the tee and achieve the best position. The second shot on a par-5 is easy. You will not be able to reach the green so there is no pressure.

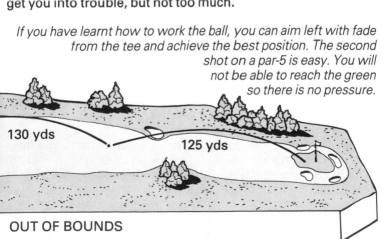

130 yds

125 yds

OUT OF BOUNDS

Looking towards the green. To the right is out-of-bounds and a bunker awaits the short approach.

A good but not strained shot should reach about 130 yards, leaving you short of these hazards and with just about 125 yards to the front of the green – the measurements on the course guide at Rungsted are to the front of the green, not the centre as on some courses.

"You need to be careful about what you are hitting from here," Bob continued. "Golf is a game of mathematics. The best courses, the older ones, were built so cunningly that every shot had to be thought about. Although course guides, with yardages laid out, or 150 metre markers on the course, are relatively new, they are so useful.

"Learn to know your distances with each club, then carefully study whatever information you have available. Trust the course guides, not your eyes – they will deceive you. Mr Average gets a shot and thinks to himself, 'That's a 4-iron' but he doesn't *know*. He neither knows how far it is nor how far he hits a 4-iron!

"The tour pros rely totally on their yardage charts and their caddies to get the distances right – using their skill to analyse wind conditions which might have an effect on the ball. If you sent Faldo, Nicklaus and a few others out without any yardage charts or course markers they would have difficulty in choosing the right club. Don't trust your eyes. If your course has no markers, pace it out. Don't just hit and hope!"

We moved to what Bob Beattie correctly calls the 'most aggressive shot in golf' – the first putt.

"This is where you really need to get the ball close enough to the hole to give you an easy second putt. Again you need to know the distance to the pin – pace it out, don't guess. That short walk also gives you a feel for whether it is uphill or down, and how soft or hard the green is. Getting the ball close enough for an easy second putt builds your confidence, and puts pressure on your opponent in a match."

As we walked off the green Bob spoke of how many players go through a patch where they are fading shots, then maybe they get straighter, then start drawing.

"It's all a matter of fine tuning, just like the radio volume. You need perhaps to very slightly turn your grip one way or the other to get it just right. Is it a bit too loud, a fraction too low. You adjust it without thinking about it. Learn to do the same with your golf shots. *Feel* them. Understand them."

The first putt should be paced out. Don't just guess the distance.

East Sussex National, UK
Bob Cupp, Course Architect

12th hole, 548 yards

St Andrews, The Belfry, Troon and Wentworth are all well-known and respected courses in Britain which, between them, regularly host some of the major British championship tournaments. However, there is another course that might soon rank equal billing alongside these famous names: East Sussex National.

Horsted Place, a fine nineteenth-century English country house, sits splendidly in the Sussex countryside not far from Uckfield, a few miles from Glyndebourne, home of the famous summer opera festival. The house looks out on the Sussex Downs, verdant rolling hills which extend along the south coast of England. Until his death in 1982, the house was owned by Lord Nevill, private secretary to Prince Philip. The Prince, accompanied by Queen Elizabeth, was a frequent weekend visitor to the house. In 1984 it was sold to a Canadian company, Granfel, headed by Brian Turner.

In the grounds of Horsted Place, Granfel is in the process of

Horsted Place has fine facilities.

The intimidating view from the tee. The drive needs to clear both the bushes and the creek before reaching the safety of the fairway. Making a birdie is very difficult.

creating Europe's first custom-built stadium golf course, very similar to those on the TPC circuit in the United States.

Conduits for television cables, electricity for hospitality units alongside some of the greens, together with all the other facilities needed for a major golf tournament have been built into the course. An exclusive country club and a top-class hotel are being built on the 11,000-acre site; two championship quality courses, each measuring 7,100 yards, and a golf academy, featuring a driving range and a three-hole practice circuit, are all part of the complex.

Course construction began in May 1988, and the official opening of the two courses took place in April 1990 (the hotel will be ready in 1992). The main championship course will be the 'East' course, with hillocks and terraces built into the course layout for spectators – 50,000 people can safely watch the climax around the last green!

On the Monday before Christmas, with the course still closed to any but a few invited guests, I went to try out one of the most testing par-5s, the 548-yard 12th on the West course, a devil of a dog-leg with a long tee shot and a tight approach to the green.

I was fortunate enough to be accompanied, not on this occasion by the pro, but by the course architect, Bob Cupp, who came along to explain how he had designed the hole to test the best golfers. His design is intended to test the professionals, yet lesser mortals like you and me are given the opportunity to play it from a forward tee, taking out some of the difficulty of the first shot, yet still making the hole a challenge.

With Nick Green, Marketing Manager of the club (and a mean 3-handicapper himself) as my playing partner (and caddy) we went out in one of the worst rain-storms I can remember. Fortunately I was wearing waterproofs and wet-weather shoes, which kept me both dry and warm!

The hole, from the 'gold' (championship) tee, measures 548 yards, although members will normally play from either of the forward tees, at 519 or 501 yards. Bob Cupp explained the features of the hole.

"The men's tees play across Little Horsted Creek, an expanse of 100 yards at this point where it joins the River Uck. However, it is not all water except when the river is in flood. At other times it is marshy, but when it is really dry you can play out of it."

Nick and I played from the 'blue' tee, at 519 yards, where the tee shot needs to rise over some bushes and carry the creek, some 150 yards carry, before reaching the safety of the fairway. Nothing less than a full shot is safe here.

Two bunkers, at the professional driving distance, sit on a slight incline on the right of the fairway, about 230 yards from

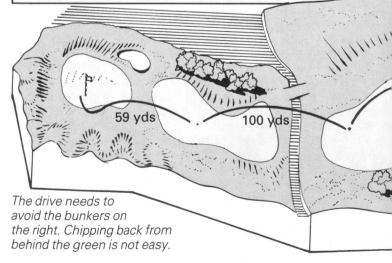

East Sussex National

- **Courses are carefully designed and it pays to study them seriously**

59 yds   100 yds

The drive needs to avoid the bunkers on the right. Chipping back from behind the green is not easy.

our tee. I was short. My partner just clipped the edge of one of the bunkers.

"These two bunkers," Bob Cupp continued, "show the best position for the drive." This is why he put them there: to draw the tee shot into danger. A good player, having reached this area, will not have much opportunity to reach the green in two.

"The second shot, if played from the right side, provides the best angle into the sloping, second landing area." This is across the creek that winds alongside the hole, and that twice crosses it.

"Safer tee shots away from those two bunkers, to the left, will cause the player to be more cautious with the second shot, or be forced to hit a left-to-right to avoid the slopes on the left.

"The green itself sits just above the creek at the top of a high bank which includes a six-foot deep grass bunker. Although the approach is kept in rough grass, it is possible to bounce the ball along the sharply rising left front edge of the green. The large putting surface is easily visible for a long approach shot. However, the entire back of the green is a large grassy hollow. Chipping back to the green will be chancy because the green slopes fairly dramatically towards the creek on the right."

The wayward approach left, away from the greenside bunker and creek on the right, could land on one of the slopes on the left, leaving an even more difficult chip. Once the ball lands on the green it will just roll to the lower edge, leaving a long putt uphill to the pin.

Having hit a good drive, Nick played a long 2-iron off the

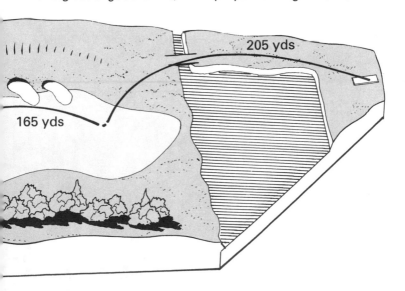

205 yds

165 yds

fairway to carry the creek that crosses the fairway. He then played a 9-iron approach shot to the back of the green, leaving two putts for a five. I, having been shorter on the drive but slightly more left, laid-up in front of the creek as it crosses the fairway, then hit a 5-iron to the approach area. My wedge to the green stayed too far left, leaving me with a downhill chip into the putting surface. Inevitably the ball rolled down and it took two putts to get home, for a seven. With my handicap and the hole's index, that was not quite good enough for a net par. Yet, as is so obvious, you have to know where you are going on a course, and then to plan your strategy, rather than just blasting away and hoping to get as close to the flag as possible.

Courses are not designed like a driving range, a huge flat expanse of open space at which to aim. They are carefully constructed with trees, bunkers, slopes, water, rough and narrow areas, to force the golfer to manoeuvre the ball from tee to green. I had not given enough thought to golf course design until then when I saw how an expert used all his skill and cunning to make the hole difficult – yet perfectly playable.

The last word comes from Bob Cupp himself: ''This is a spectacular hole, winding along the creek, and setting up three fully visible challenges. Played conservatively it offers little resistance to par. But making a birdie is a different matter!''

Looking towards the green. An accurate tee shot will allow the second to reach the 'approach' position or to be laid-up short.

Meon Valley, UK
John Stirling, Club Professional

1st hole, 476 yards

Nestling down in a gently rolling valley in Hampshire, not far from Southampton, is the Meon Valley Country Club, with its splendid hotel and well-planned golf course. The complex, which is well utilized by companies holding conferences and golf days, is run by the same organization that operates St Pierre in Chepstow, the course that hosts the Epson Grand Prix.

The club pro is John Stirling, one of the most respected teachers of golf in the United Kingdom. He held the Captaincy of the PGA in 1989 – Ryder Cup year. John is also the National Coach for the English Golf Union, and is much sought after for his patient and well-proven coaching skills.

John Stirling, Professional at Meon Valley; a highly respected teacher and National Coach for the English Golf Union.

We met on a glorious summer morning and stood on the first tee shortly after eight o'clock, the sun glinting across the dew-laden turf. The first hole is a challenging par-5, 476 yards from the yellow tee, which we decided to play. The medal tee gives the hole a distance of 484 yards, and the Ladies have a 424-yard challenge. True to form, half a dozen regular members were watching intently as I gazed into the misty distance.

The hole slopes away from the tee, heading downhill with a slope from left to right, so the fade that seems naturally to come to the average player like myself would be exaggerated, pushing the ball further right than I really wanted. Down the left is a line of trees and an out-of-bounds line, separating the fairway from the practice ground. The hole then turns left and narrows, dipping into a hollow and crossing a stream, before climbing to a raised green, guarded by two bunkers at the front. The pin on this day was cut to the left and, with a green depth (front to back) of thirty yards, was set about ten yards from the back, giving a total playing distance of about 480 yards.

"The way to play this hole," my partner and teacher told me, "is *from the pin back*. The major hazard, apart from the two bunkers which are close in on the green, is the stream which runs across, eighty yards from the pin.

"You have to set the hole up to ensure that your third shot will be from about twenty yards short of this stream, allowing you to float the ball up over the bunkers and onto the green for two putts and a par, or net birdie.

"It is also the first hole, and we are all 'cold' and nervous on the first tee. The suggestion I would make, therefore, is that you don't try to overhit the first shot, but go more for direction, using a 3-wood or a 1-iron if you prefer. I would leave the driver in the bag for this shot."

I heeded his advice and took the 3-wood (although for a

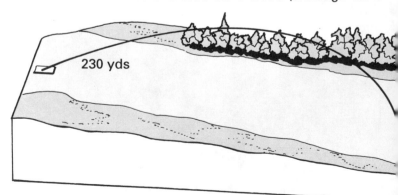

230 yds

player who can handle a 1-iron effectively that would be a good choice). I teed the ball low and, having made a few practice swings, stepped up and struck my first shot of the morning. Realizing that I tended to push the ball right, I aimed down the left of the fairway, close in to the trees, but not so close that I might hit any of them. The ball flew away through the mist, landing dead centre on the fairway, which at this point is fairly wide. The distance was 230 yards – quite pleasing for the first of the morning.

As we walked down feeling the first warming rays of the sun gleaming through the mist, John reminded me that the stroke index on this hole was 11, so my aim for 'par' was 6, not 5.

"Too many players plan their round without taking their handicap into account," he said. "Handicaps are the great equalizer, so you should *always use up the allowance you have been given*. That's the clever way to play golf."

The second shot left me blind to the hole, trees coming in from the right blocking the view.

Meon Valley

- **Plan each hole from the pin back**
- **A good first hole sets up the rest of your round**
- **Don't overhit your shot on the first tee**
- **Plan your round taking your handicap fully into account**

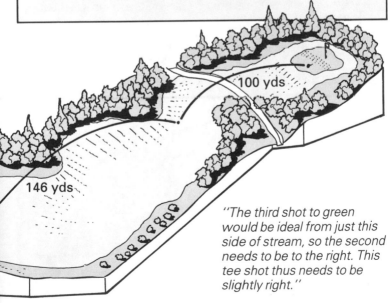

100 yds

146 yds

"The third shot to green would be ideal from just this side of stream, so the second needs to be to the right. This tee shot thus needs to be slightly right."

"From there your one aim is to lay-up short of the stream," John reminded me. "The distance to the stream is 167 yards, but you really don't want to dice with death going too close to it. Choose a club that will get you 135–145 yards, leaving you a good 20 yards short. As the ground slopes down to the stream, any ball will roll, particularly if the ground is very dry and hard."

I chose a 6-iron and aimed for a point well left of the direct line to the flag, aware that the ball would roll right as it started on the downslope to the water. The shot flew well and pitched nicely, settling down just before the slope gets too steep, which would leave an unpleasant downhill lie. The distance left was just over 100 yards, giving me 146 yards with that 6-iron, again fine for this early in the round. Later, perhaps, a 7-iron might have carried the same distance, but John stressed the importance of not straining too much this early in a round and of taking the club with which you can reach easily, not the one that could only reach only if you hit the perfect shot.

The third shot left me 100 yards direct to the pin, but fairly steeply uphill and from a slightly downhill lie. I chose a 7-iron and swung easily, landing the shot fifteen inches from the pin for a careful putt to give me a birdie, but a net 'eagle' – four points in a stableford! Without planning it from the pin backwards, as John had suggested, I would probably have

The second shot is here blind to the hole with trees on the right blocking the view. A 6-iron of about 140 yards will leave the ball a good 20 yards short of the stream. Early in the round it is most important not to overstrain and make an over-ambitious choice of club. Play within yourself.

*Playing the approach shot
to the green, after laying up.*

worked the ball totally differently and have been lucky to hit a
gross six. Even so, as John pointed out, that would have been
good enough for a net 'par'.

By thinking about your golf, rather than blindly trying to hit
the ball as far as possible, you can achieve a more satisfactory
result, particularly on the first hole. A good result early sets you
up mentally for the rest of your round.

*A solid 3-wood off the tee will put the ball into the right position for
the second shot, which needs to be laid-up and which is blind. The
approach shot is then made considerably easier.*

Waterville, Republic of Ireland
Liam Higgins, Club Professional

11th hole, 538 yards

"Don't stand over the ball thinking about birdies and pars – get on with your game and they'll come along on their own!"

This good advice came from Liam Higgins, the long-hitting professional at Waterville Golf Club, in the south-west corner of Ireland.

Golf has been played at Waterville since the mid-nineteenth century when the village became the eastern base for the giant trans-Atlantic submarine telephone cables being laid between Europe and the United States. However, the course as it exists today is fairly new, having been constructed to the wishes of John A Mulcahy, an Irish-American who came here in the early 1970s and spent considerable time, effort and money in producing a fine course which must surely soon play host to a major championship.

Inevitably the course is subjected to the howling winds that screech across Ballinnskelligs Bay off the Atlantic Ocean.

On the day we went out the wind was measuring a mere 6.9 on the Beaufort scale, but fortunately it was behind us so, as Liam advised, the only thing to do was 'to use it'.

We started on the 11th hole, a 538-yard par-5 named, for no obvious reason, 'Tranquillity', a hole that Gary Player once described as the most beautiful par-5 in the world.

The hole runs down a man-made valley, cutting the player off

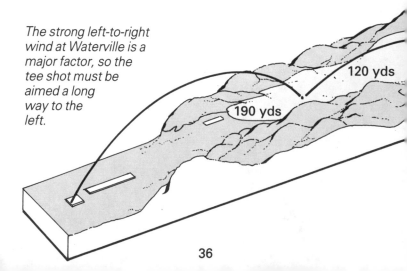

The strong left-to-right wind at Waterville is a major factor, so the tee shot must be aimed a long way to the left.

120 yds

190 yds

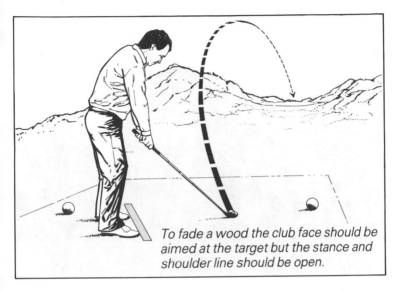

To fade a wood the club face should be aimed at the target but the stance and shoulder line should be open.

from the outside world, although from the tee the elements are very much in evidence. The wind was howling in from the sea, blowing across the tee both from left to right and from behind.

"Aim a long way left," advised Liam. "Stand slightly open with the ball more in the centre of the stance than you normally would for a tee shot. You must also aim, on every tee shot, to knock the tee-peg out of the ground — that will ensure you are hitting through the lower part of the ball, getting it airborne and

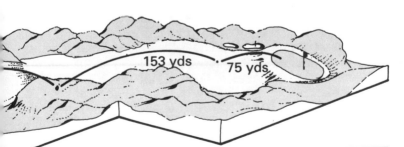

153 yds   75 yds

Waterville

- Concentrate on hitting the fairway rather than on distance
- Concentrate on your game rather than birdies and pars
- With a fairway wood hit the *centre* of the ball
- In high winds, *use* the wind

Sam Snead, with good reason, called Waterville 'The Magnificent Monster'. The drive is critical on every hole and wayward shots are punished either by rough or by water. Above is the fairway of the beautiful 11th hole.

putting sufficient spin on it to get distance.''

Liam certainly knows about distance off the tee for he has hit a ball a massive 638 yards, and, in a contest in 1986, hit a ball an amazing 310-yard carry across water!

''Let the wind bring the ball round,'' he then advised me.

It certainly did. I aimed, with a 3-wood, far to the left, way off the fairway. Sure enough the wind brought it round and the valley did the rest, settling the ball into the middle of the fairway. A 3-wood again was the best choice off the fairway, with Liam emphasising that you must 'brush the club through the grass, keeping it as low as possible for as long as possible.'

He explained that with a fairway wood you hit the *centre* of the ball, not the bottom as you do with an iron.

''You must hit through the centre of the ball,'' he pointed out. ''If you hit the top, that will take off distance. Hit the bottom and you will dig into the ground and restrict the follow-through. By hitting the middle of the ball you push it forward further in a flatter trajectory.''

In order to practise this, just keep swinging a club through some long grass, just to feel how the club has to be pulled through low and long.

The wind was not apparent in the valley but as the ball rose the wind caught it and sent it flying to the right, landing on one of the hills on the side of the fairway. Fortunately it was not sitting too badly, although the shot was very awkward, the ball being at least two feet above my feet and on a very steep side slope.

It was obvious that I would have to grip right down the club to 'shorten' it, grasping it at the very bottom of the grip. I needed some distance from here so I had taken a 5-iron. I also remembered something about aiming left — or was it right? — with the ball above the feet, and right, or maybe left, with the ball below the feet.

"When the ball is above the feet," Liam put me right, "aim right, with the club face open. When the ball is below the feet, close the face and aim left."

The thing to remember is that the ball will go with the slope, so hit against the slope. That will get the ball straight.

I aimed what I thought was a long way right, gripped down and kept the body still, only swinging with the arms, with very little shoulder turn. Any excessive movement here will tip you off balance, so stay as still as you can.

The ball flew off straight as an arrow, landing safely back on the fairway. The approach from here was through that very narrow valley, with about 75 yards to run. The green is elevated so a high shot was needed to get on the back of the green. A sand wedge did the trick, with the aim to the left again to let the wind work the ball, which it did, bringing it round to sit down on the green for a two-putt and a six.

Going off the fairway had cost me the par, which just went to emphasise Liam's earlier advice on strategy.

"Just concentrate on keeping the ball on the fairway — that way you will drop fewer shots than the big hitter who can't hit the ball straight."

(Left) When the ball is above your feet then the club face must be open.
(Right) But if the ball is below feet then the club face must be closed.

Royal Waterloo, Belgium
George Will, Club Professional

17th hole, 524 yards

In 1815, Napoleon, after escaping from Elba, tried to smash the combined forces of the British and Prussians by attacking them on France's northern borders. Taken by surprise, the British, under Wellington, retreated towards Brussels to regroup, setting up camp just south of the tiny village of Waterloo.

Napoleon attacked at noon on June 18th but after a bloody battle in which 55,000 died, was defeated and banished to St. Helena.

On the site today stands a huge monument, visible for miles around. Very close to it, on part of that huge battlefield, is one of the courses of the Royal Waterloo Golf Club, 'Le Lion'. The main championship course, 'La Marache', is more hilly, with a protected hollow. It was in this very hollow that Wellington's men set up camp before the battle. Players on the course today stand, literally, in Wellington's footsteps. The 'battles' these days are the Belgian Open, the Godiva ladies' tournament and the European Amateur event.

Overlooking the scene is the club professional and one of the

---

Royal Waterloo

- **On a par-5, decide from where you want to hit the third shot and work back from there**
- **Pay careful attention to the stroke index on each hole and judge the shots on the conditions of the day**
- **Avoid using the driver**
- **With a 3-wood, tee the ball with the top of the club level to the ball's equator**

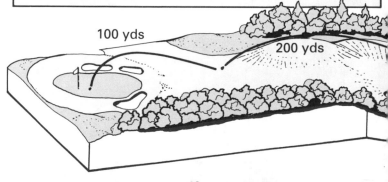

100 yds

200 yds

George Will, coach to the Belgian National Team.

most influential people in Belgian golf, ex-Ryder Cup player George Will, who also represented his native Scotland in the World Cup in the 1960s. He is now National Coach to the Royal Belgian Golf Federation and takes a very keen interest in the development of golf in the country.

"In the four years since I've been here," he told me, "the number of golf courses in Belgium has doubled and there are now about 30,000 active golfers, most of whom are very keen to take lessons to learn this great game."

Over 1,400 of them belong to the Royal Waterloo, thus coming under George's expert guidance. I became one of them for an afternoon to learn how to play the 524-yard, par-5 17th.

"The first thing," he told me as we stood on the tee which is just outside the club-house, "is to avoid using the driver. Far

"Be sensible and plan your route to the green. Avoid all the hazards along the way. Give yourself a chance!"

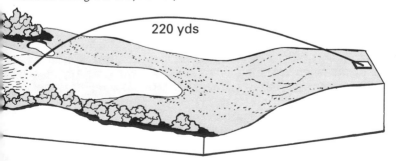

220 yds

"Slicers tee too low; hookers tee too high; the correct height is with the top of the club by the equator of the ball."

too many people reach for the driver automatically; most play better without it.

"For most long holes the average player would be better off hitting two three-woods, giving him control and the same distance as a drive and an iron. Work out the distances and split them in half rather than thinking that you need to make seventy-five per cent of the distance on the first shot!

"On this hole, if you can hit two 220-yard shots all you're left with is a pitch in with an 8-iron or less. Getting on in two is very difficult because of the bunkers around the right side of the green and the way the fairway slopes from right to left.

"Hitting a 3-wood off the tee allows you more control on direction and that is the thing to think of – too many players just want to hit long. I suggest they hit straight!"

Teeing the ball for a 3-wood shot produced an interesting discussion about faults that arise from teeing the ball either too high or too low. George demonstrated how high to tee the ball for a 3-wood, with the top of the club about level with the equator of the ball.

"You can often tell whether a player hooks or slices," George told me, "by the height he tees the ball. Most faders tee it too low, most of those who hook tee it too high. Think of what happens when the ball is on a sideslope, with it below the level of your feet. The ball is too low for a correct swing into it and so fades right. When it's above your feet, and thus too high, it hooks left. It's the same on the tee!

"Most amateurs tee it too low, when the angle of attack of the club is less effective and sidespin takes over more. You thus stand more chance of hitting it correctly if you tee a little higher.

"The other major point to take into account," he continued, "is the grip, which again is not paid as much attention as it should be by most players. The hands have to be facing each other – they have to be matched like two halves of a shell."

He showed me the correct grip by holding the club in the left hand, balanced finely between the first finger and the pad on the hand opposite the thumb.

"This ensures balance of the club and the correct grip. Once you have got the club in this position, just grip with the rest of the fingers; then slide the right hand into position, getting as 'tight' onto the left hand as possible."

I explained that I did not favour the interlocking or Vardon grip where the little finger of the right hand overlays the left hand. Having small hands I feel, rightly or wrongly, that I lose control and power if I do overlap the fingers. George allayed my worries.

"That's not so important. It's the *front* of the grip that is really important."

I took up the grip he had shown me, but he pushed my hands further together, almost as if they should be touching at the wrists, but obviously with the left hand lower down (when looked at 'upside down'). As with any grip adjustment it felt strange at first but is something to which you quickly get accustomed. It now feels perfectly normal.

We aimed the tee shot slightly right, to avoid the right-to-left slope on the fairway which would take the ball into trouble. There are bunkers on the right but these are not in reach off the tee, being 280 yards forward. The ball ended up on a slight upward incline, making the second shot, with the same 3-wood, easier to get airborne.

"You must always, on a par-5, decide from where you want

"To hit 300 yards, is it easier to hit one enormous shot and one tiny one; or two easy ones?"

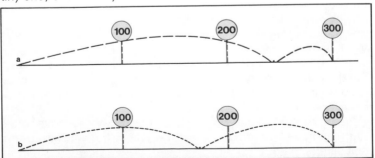

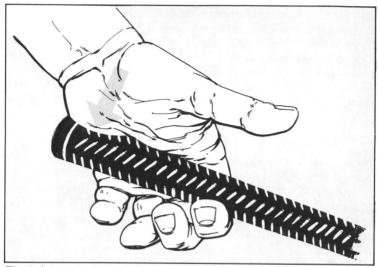

The left hand grip is vital – base of index finger to pad opposite thumb. You should be able to balance the club this way.

to hit the third shot," George told me. "Work back from there.

"It's also vital to know how far you hit each club. Professionals know to within a yard – be able to judge yours to within ten. Measure them on the practice area and on the course as you go round – get to know what you can hit and then use it.

"The same goes for your normal type of shot – if you always fade, use it. Aim left and work the ball round into position.

"You must also use your handicap rather than trying to par the course's handicap. Use the strokes you have, and pay careful attention to the stroke index on each hole – it's not there by accident but is designed to let you know, in advance, how difficult the hole is likely to be. The lower the index the harder the hole. Look at the scorecard carefully before teeing off so you know what you're up against, and judge the shots on today's conditions – not on what you hit last week – the wind may have changed direction today."

Golfers in Belgium are keen to take lessons and improve, which is exciting for the game in that country, and true too of several other parts of mainland Europe. George makes sure that they all spend some time on the putting green, too, for, as he so rightly says, "That is the only time on a golf course when you score – once that ball drops.

"If you can't hit a ball off the tee, or putt it, you'll never play golf. You have to start and finish. Dictate to the course – don't let it dictate to you!"

The Belfry, UK
Peter McGovern, Club Professional

15th hole, 540 yards

The Belfry, located not far from Birmingham, was the venue for the 1985 and 1989 Ryder Cup matches between Europe and the United States. It was also the first golf course that I visited, as a press guest on the last day of the 1985 Ryder Cup, although it was another year before I ventured out onto a golf course with a half set of clubs.

Once a potato field, The Belfry is now one of the premier inland courses in England, with a testing variety of holes including that famous, or perhaps infamous, par-4 18th. Its two long shots over the water have claimed many victims, including several top pros in the 1989 Ryder Cup matches.

I played the difficult, long 15th, a 540-yard par-5 which runs downhill from the tee after crossing a path, then uphill over a stream to the green. An interesting feature of the hole is the undulating terrain on the left of the fairway, giving the slightly wayward player the opportunity to play a variety of shots off ground that is anything but level. To the right is a long, flat bunker, from which escape can very easily bring the stream into play.

My teacher on this hole was the Club Professional Peter McGovern, who bears a striking resemblance in both build and

The Club Professional at The Belfry is Peter McGovern.

features to Ian Woosnam. A few days after the conclusion of the 1989 Ryder Cup matches we went out on the course.

The shot from the tee is relatively easy. Distance is at a premium because the closer to the stream you are, the better. The path is cleared with a shot of just 160 yards and the bunker on the left comes into play after 238 yards. But with the average player's tendency to slice and the fact that the hole is a slight dog-leg left, the bunker on the right, at 266 yards, is more likely to be a factor if the ball is struck well and the ground hard.

We hit three tee shots to try to land them off the centre of the fairway. One landed in the bunker on the right and two on the 'hilly' areas on the left, which was perfect for what we wanted.

The long bunker on the right is quite flat so a less lofted club can be used to get out. Depending on the lie of the ball, anything down to a 6-iron is feasible, depending on whether you think you can carry the stream or not. From the front (closest to the green) of the bunker there is a carry of about 70 yards to clear that hazard. If in doubt, lay up with a 9-iron or wedge ready for a good third shot across to the approach to the green. Once again it is a matter of getting into position for the next shot, like a good chess or snooker player.

Landing on the left of the fairway presents other interesting situations, with side-lies and sloping lies. Peter demonstrated how best to play shots like these.

The first example was with the ball on a downslope, some

The Belfry, UK

- On a side-slope with the ball below feet, close the club face
- Treat long iron shots from the fairway like normal shots, aiming the body straight at the target

250 yds

The huge bunker on the right will trap many drives, so a shot slightly left will be the safe choice.

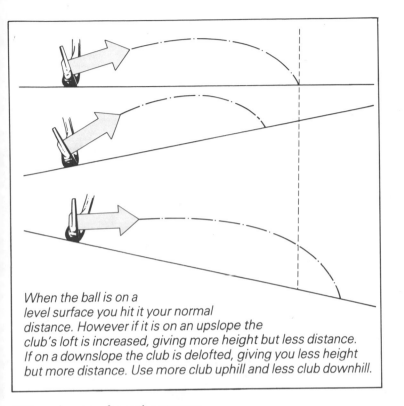

*When the ball is on a
level surface you hit it your normal
distance. However if it is on an upslope the
club's loft is increased, giving more height but less distance.
If on a downslope the club is delofted, giving you less height
but more distance. Use more club uphill and less club downhill.*

100 yards away from the stream.

"With the ball on a downslope the body would naturally try to right itself, which puts more weight on the right foot as you compensate for the slope," Peter explained. "Unfortunately this means that you are leaning away from the ball and will tend to hit too much under it, either scooping it high and short, or, more likely, topping it.

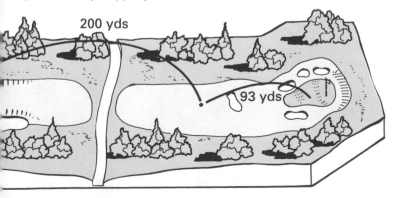

200 yds

93 yds

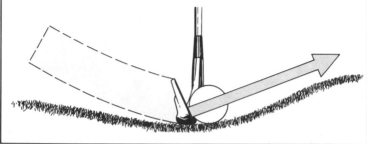

If the ball is in a hollow, use a sufficiently lofted club to get out safely and come down steeper into the back of the ball, punching it out.

"The answer is to ignore gravity and set the body up at right angles to the slope, so that you appear to be standing 'upright' as you hit the ball."

The other important aspect about a downslope is that the club is automatically 'delofted', turning a 5-iron into a 3, for example. The ball will thus stay lower so if there are hazards in the way a more lofted club might be necessary – unfortunately that reduces distance.

Because of the angle of the slope, and the fact that more weight is now on the left foot, the ball should be positioned further back in the stance, by about a foot. This, together with a slightly steeper backswing than normal, will bring the club down firmer on the back of the ball, getting it airborne faster.

The approach shot to the green on the 15th, which is guarded by no less than five bunkers.

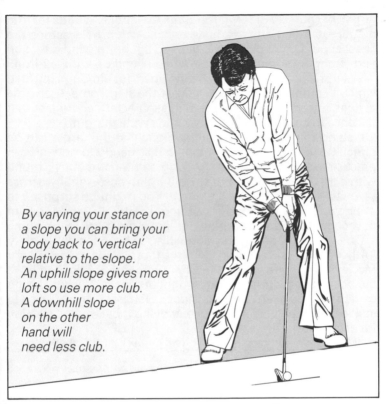

By varying your stance on a slope you can bring your body back to 'vertical' relative to the slope. An uphill slope gives more loft so use more club. A downhill slope on the other hand will need less club.

Should the ball be on a downslope in a hollow, this is even more important.

The third ball had landed on a side-slope where it was below the feet.

"This kind of shot needs a closed face," Peter explained, "because a ball below the feet will always veer right, going with the slope. By closing the face you aim it left — the slope compensates and it then flies straight."

Closing the club face enough to compensate for the slope is just a matter of practice — nobody can teach you. As I had discovered at Waterville a few weeks earlier, a ball above the feet should be played with an open club face, aiming it right where the slope compensates and bringimg it round straight.

"Long iron shots (that's when you *do* land on the fairway!) are very easy," Peter tried to convince me.

"All you need to do is treat them as normal golf shots, aiming the body straight at the target."

On some short shots it often helps to stand 'open' to get height on the ball, adjusting the club face to hit towards the target, of course. For long iron shots (or fairway woods for that matter) standing straight is essential. A club held across the chest should point directly at the flag (ignoring wind direction and strength for the moment). When I lined up with a 2-iron I was surprised to find I was standing open, for although my feet, which I could see, were pointing at the flag some 160 yards distant, my shoulders were aiming slightly left, enough at that distance to hook the ball left by a fairly wide margin.

Getting the shoulders pointing directly at the target can be difficult and is one of those things that needs to be learnt in practice sessions. If you are playing a non-competitive round with a friend get him or her to hold a club occasionally across your chest to check your alignment. You might be surprised to see how far left your body is aiming! I certainly was, and I am now concentrating on turning the shoulders more to the right.

One other way of aligning correctly is to have the ball slightly further back (i.e. towards the right foot) in the stance. Peter McGovern suggests that the way to remember this is to have the ball left of centre for woods, right of centre for irons, taking care to vary the stance from inside the left heel for a 1-wood to inside the right heel for a wedge, moving it back a tiny fraction for each club.

"Unless you aim straight, you will never hit straight!"

To test if you are standing square, a club held across the chest should point directly towards the flag. For long irons you must be square. Here the right hand V is too far right.

Sleepy Hollow, New York State, USA
Jim McLean, Club Professional

6th hole, 457 yards

Sleepy Hollow is not as well known as many other courses on either side of the Atlantic. It is hardly surprising, for this historical club on the banks of the Hudson some 40 miles up-river from New York City actively shuns publicity. Yet on the 16th it has one of the most awe-inspiring views to be found anywhere in the world of golf.

It also has, in club professional Jim McLean, one of the leading lights in teaching golf in the United States.

Jim McLean is keen to see a more formal approach to the blooding of young men who wish to become club pro-fessionals; the USA has different standards to those pertaining in Europe. However, that is a long-term task – for now Jim is one of the most interesting teachers in American golf, although in a very quiet, modest way.

On a misty November morning, but one that later turned out

Club Professional at Sleepy Hollow is Jim McLean, a popular teacher. Jim recommends the little-used 7-wood.

to be brilliant, sunny and warm, we visited one of the most intriguing par-5s I have come across, the 457-yard 6th.

The tee is elevated, giving the false sense of security that, with a good drive, you can clear the deep valley in front of the tee and carry to the temptingly close – or is it? – ridge where the hole dog-legs sharply right.

"Treat this as a genuine three-shot par-5," Jim warned me as we stood on the tee. "The steep uphill begins at about 175 yards off the tee and to get to the top of the hill you need a safe carry of over 225 yards – not too many amateur players can achieve that. For the longer hitters the problem, if they do carry it, is that they run out of fairway because the hole turns right.

"For the average player the safest way to play the hole is to take something short off the tee, like a 5-wood or 7-wood, and sit the ball down in the hollow going slightly left if anything so that you make more of an angle on the corner."

Jim suggested that not enough players recognise from which side of the tee they should be hitting, nor do they understand sufficiently how high or low to tee the ball for a 5- or 7-wood.

"When you have an angle on a hole to get round you need to give yourself the widest possible hitting area. For example, here, the hole turns right and there are trees the entire length of

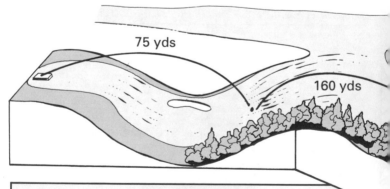

75 yds

160 yds

Sleepy Hollow

- Work out from which side of the tee you should be hitting
- Tee very low when using a 5- or 7-wood from the tee. A 7-wood will hit roughly the same distance as most people hit a 4-iron
- With a blind shot, fix on a landmark as a guide
- Know how far you hit your shots

the right side of the fairway. You therefore need to be hitting to the left to give yourself enough room to get round the corner. The best place to stand is on the far right of the tee so that you can hit across the fairway.

"When you are using a 5- or 7-wood from the tee you also want to tee it very low, almost pushing the peg in as far as possible, with just the cup above ground."

I felt more comfortable hitting a 4-iron (just a personal choice – I feel more comfortable with longer irons) to the hollow, aiming left.

The next shot is totally blind, a 70-foot incline between you and your third shot. I walked to the top of the hill and looked for what I thought was a safe landing area, to give a direct line into the green. The centre of the fairway here is very safe. It is essential, when you have a 'blind' shot, to be able to fix on some landmark as a guide, rather than just vaguely hoping the green is 'thataway'. I positioned myself between the ball and my next target and fixed on a tree on the skyline which I could keep in view. That way I knew I was aiming in approximately the right direction.

Going back to the ball, Jim told me that to get up an incline like this, a fairly lofted club was essential. His recommendation was for a club not in my bag, nor, I would imagine, to be found in many golf bags in Europe – a *7-wood.*.

"This really is a wonderful club to use, particularly for high

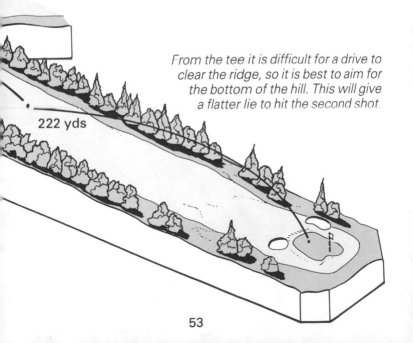

From the tee it is difficult for a drive to clear the ridge, so it is best to aim for the bottom of the hill. This will give a flatter lie to hit the second shot.

222 yds

handicappers, Senior players and Ladies," he told me. "It is easy to swing, being not too long, and has fine loft which gets the ball up in the air very quickly. That helps build confidence more than anything, because if you hit a high shot you feel more successful. Rolling a shot along the fairway might get it there if the course is dry but doesn't feel as good as hitting high. You can also, of course, control the distance better and stop the ball faster if it's hit high.

"The 7-wood will also hit roughly the same distance as most people can strike a 4-iron."

I used the next best thing, a 5-wood and got the ball safely up the hill and onto the flat area of fairway, leaving me a clear shot to the green, with about 150 yards to go.

Jim now raised the subject of distance. "How far," he asked, "do you hit a 5-iron?" I hesitated and guessed about 150 yards.

"And how far do you hit a 3-wood?"

I looked bemused.

"Knowing how far you hit shots is of vital importance," he told me. "Be aware of the average length that you regularly achieve with each club so you can plan your course strategy much better.

"For example, if you have 200 yards to go off the fairway you will need two shots. What do you take – a 3-wood and a pitch, or a 5-iron and a 9? Which is easier to control? Think carefully, know your distances and split shots up into controllable, manageable distances where you know you can hit the target. Don't try necessarily to get as close as possible with the first shot. A longer pitch into the green is probably easier than a

When using a 5- or 7-wood from the tee, make sure that the ball is teed at the correct height. Push the peg in as far as possible so that the cup is only just above ground.

The view looking back from the hill towards the tee. The aiming point should be the fairway (arrowed). When playing up a blind incline, it is helpful to select an appropriate landmark to aim by.

short one — you can get the ball higher and thus control it as it comes down."

I took the 5-iron and hit it straight, to the front fringe of the green. Jim had warned me that, with the green sloping back to front, the place to miss the pin was short, leaving an uphill putt.

I hooded a 9-iron and just chipped it towards the flag for what should have left me an easy putt for a par. I won't tell you how many I actually took but I can tell you that greens in the United States are fast, and I mean *fast!*

Jim concluded by advising that players should spend time learning how to play one hole on their course. Get the pro to give you a lesson on one particular hole, be it a par-5, 4, or 3.

"That way you get to understand strategy," he said. "Also, when you face a difficult tee shot, when there's a hazard in front of the tee, or on the first tee, when you haven't quite warmed up and there's a crowd of people watching you, take a really comfortable club. Ignore that driver, reach for the 7-wood, or 5-iron or something. Just knock it straight down the middle of the fairway. You'll probably surprise yourself with the distance that you achieve."

And with that last piece of advice he dashed off to give a lesson to one of the Rockefeller clan on the family's private 18-hole golf course nearby.

Kingston Heath GC, Melbourne, Australia
Leonard Sorensen, Club Professional

12th hole, 485 yards

Any golf course chosen as one of the sites of the Australian Open and other major Tour events, must be a challenge, and so it is with Kingston Heath, to the south of Melbourne. The course was laid out in 1925 but due to a disastrous bush fire in 1944 that destroyed much of it, some adjustments were made before today's beautiful, but challenging course finally came into being.

The professional today is Leonard Sorensen, who chose for our lesson the testing par-5 12th, 442 metres (485 yards) off the championship tee.

"The main priority on the tee-shot," he said as we stood in the late afternoon January sun, "is to avoid the bunkers on the fairway 207 metres (227 yards) out."

The fairway here is at its widest but only begins 180 metres off the tee. Any shorter than that and you're in deep rough. The rough is a major hazard so you should stay straight for safety.

"The right of the bunkers is easier for the average player. Going straight over is fine for the player who can carry 220

Kingston Heath GC, Melbourne
- To check you are swinging correctly, put two clubs down either side of the ball, aiming at your target. Then check the direction of your divot

150 m

120 m

The fairways here are fairly narrow, so accuracy is really much more important than length.

metres (240 yards) or so, but anyone shorter must go right.''

As I got ready to address the ball he suggested that I adjust my stance to extend my arms out slightly, so that I was stretching just a little for the ball.

''This keeps the arms, as they swing, clear of the body, allowing them to swing right through.''

A word of warning here: do not overstretch or you will lose your balance. To achieve exactly the right posture will also need fine-tuning on the practice ground.

I hit a 3-wood, getting it nicely situated 200 metres (220 yards) off the tee, level with the bunkers.

''The second shot, from here, needs to be laid-up just beyond the bunkers on the left, but before those on the right.''

This meant a shot of 150 metres (165 yards), which, in the

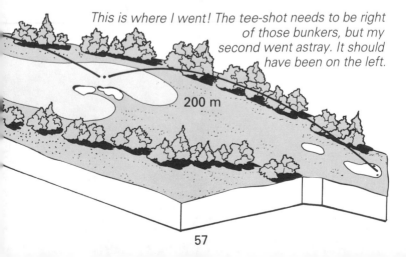

This is where I went! The tee-shot needs to be right of those bunkers, but my second went astray. It should have been on the left.

200 m

hot, dry weather and with the ball sitting up nicely on the Australian couch (pronounced 'kooch') grass, was achievable with a 4-iron. Unfortunately, I pushed it out to the right a little, just into that deadly rough.

Dropping another ball, Leonard now showed me what I had done wrong.

"Your club face and feet were perfectly aligned," he told me reassuringly, placing a club on the ground to indicate the line that I had correctly taken.

"But your shoulders and hips were turned *right*, exactly towards where the ball ended. Try, once you have the club-face and your feet aligned, turning your shoulders very slightly open, and then your hips, too.

"You will feel that you are standing open, aiming left, but trial and error tuning in practice will get it correct.

"The best way to check if you are swinging (and thus standing) correctly, is to put two clubs down either side of the ball, aiming at your target. Then check the direction of your divot. That will tell you your swing path through the ball.

"A lot of people talk about railway lines and thinking that you're aiming down them. The only problem with that is that railway lines don't meet in the distance. They only seem to.

Check that not only your feet are aligned to the target but also your knees, hips and shoulders. They must all be in line.

Lay two clubs down parallel, pointing at the target. Line your feet up on the left club, and then your club-face on the right. Then step back half a pace to position the ball.

Thus if you concentrate on these lines meeting your shoulders will be in a closed position.

"Aim your shoulders slightly left of the ball's target and then you'll be correctly aligned."

I took the third shot with my original ball, sitting in the rough. I had about 120 metres (130 yards), over a 20 feet high bush, with bunkers lying along the line to the flag.

"Choose the easiest line," Leonard advised, "which is to

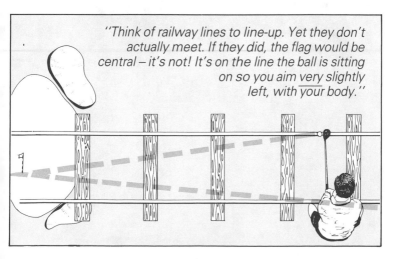

"Think of railway lines to line-up. Yet they don't actually meet. If they did, the flag would be central – it's not! It's on the line the ball is sitting on so you aim very slightly left, with your body."

come in from the front of the green, rather than gamble with the bunkers."

I set up with a 7-iron, opening the face slightly to try to bend it left to right, but still coming down steeply into the back of the ball, hacking it out of the rough.

"The important thing here, when you need to hit firmly out of rough, is to be sure not to snatch your backswing. Swing back smoothly and slowly. Put the power on – smoothly – as you come down through the ball."

The ball landed on the short-trimmed fringe, some 25 metres from the pin.

"If you have a flat, unobstructed approach on very short grass, a long putt will be as good as anything," Leonard advised me.

My long putt was not quite good enough to get down in two, on a fast green, so I ended with a six, one over.

Had the putt been better, a five would have been possible. Lining up correctly is obviously so vitally important.

"From just off the green, with nothing in the way and a flat surface, a long putt is as good as anything."

Monte Carlo
Charles Houtart, Club Professional

1st hole, 557 yards

Getting to Monte Carlo Golf Club is an experience in its own right. From the tiny Principality of Monaco the narrow road winds upwards round tight hairpin bends perched on rocky precipices that are tests of character as well as the car. Up and up you go, often into the low cloud which swirls down off the Alpes Maritimes.

At just below 3,000 feet you suddenly glimpse a green, a fairway, and then suddenly you are there. The clubhouse is imposing – sophisticated and full of enormous character and charm.

The head professional, Charles Houtart, came here in 1984 after several years on the European Tour and has made a success of teaching ever since. He took me out onto the course which hosts the Monte Carlo Open (normally the first week of July), past winners of which include Peter Senior, José Rivero, Seve Ballesteros and Mark McNulty.

The mist interfered with play on what was otherwise a perfect day as we set off down the first hole, a testing, but downhill 557-yard par-5.

"The course is built for accuracy rather than distance," Charles explained as we faced the first tee-shot, watched by a dozen local members taking lunch on the restaurant terrace. I had had the benefit of a fifteen-minute warm-up session on the

The Club Professional since 1984 at Monte Carlo is Charles Houtart, who played for many years on the European tour.

The view from the 1st tee. If the tee shot is topped it will be expensive. Trees on either side leave only a 30-yard gap through which to aim, so a well-struck shot is needed.

practice ground, just swinging a 7-iron at a bucket of balls to get the feel of the swing. If you have the facilities to do this take advantage of them. It makes so much difference to the early part of your round. Yet it is often neglected. Many players just stand by the first tee swinging a driver up and down for two minutes and then wonder why they drop shots on the first four holes.

The first real shot at Monte Carlo demands accuracy for there is nothing but very thick rough in front of the tee for 75 yards or so. Trees are on either side with a 30-yard gap to aim through. A topped shot here is very costly.

"It is, perhaps, too early to use a driver," Charles explained. "A 1-iron, well teed up, will be better." It is important to have the ball teed up well for a long iron shot, about the same height as you would for a 3-wood.

The warm-up and the correct line-up of the body did the trick, with a smooth swing connecting well, aiming slightly left down the fairway towards a bunker 270 yards away. A well-struck iron, with the advantage of the sloping ground, should carry and roll about 250 yards to the only flat part of this fairway. Local knowledge here is vital.

Going right off the tee is asking for all sorts of problems, with trees, humps, bumps and rough. The fairway is narrow, about 40 yards wide at most, so there is little room for error — rather like the road up from Monte Carlo!

The second shot, with about 290 yards to the front of the

green, needs to be aimed right, which is the only safe way to get onto the green. I was reminded of how important it is to chart the strategy on the course. Playing a course 'blind' is virtually impossible and for a visiting player a quick thirty-minute walk round will definitely pay dividends.

For the second shot, with the ball sitting well up, Charles suggested a 3-wood, to get as much distance as possible while still controlling the ball. Some players have trouble using a wood off the fairway, he added, but the answer is to treat it as you would an iron.

That second shot, aimed five yards left of the flag, will, with the slope of the fairway, come round nicely, leaving an easy (what am I saying!) third shot to the green. There is out-of-bounds at the back of this green so if you do over-hit the approach shot you have to go back to the place from where you hit, adding a penalty stroke. This can sometimes mean a long walk back so if you are in doubt you can hit a provisional ball,

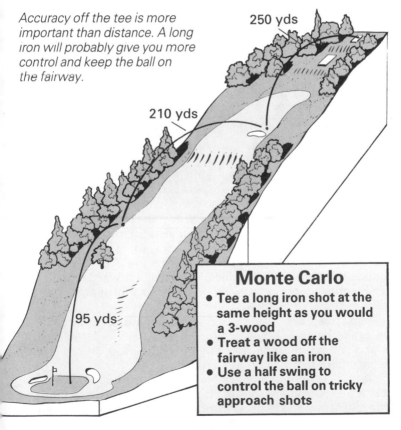

Accuracy off the tee is more important than distance. A long iron will probably give you more control and keep the ball on the fairway.

250 yds

210 yds

95 yds

Monte Carlo

- **Tee a long iron shot at the same height as you would a 3-wood**
- **Treat a wood off the fairway like an iron**
- **Use a half swing to control the ball on tricky approach shots**

With a shot which needs to 'bite' on landing, keep the left arm straight on the backswing and only cock the wrists at the last second. The club is held in the fingers, not the palm.

which will help save time if your first shot *has* gone out-of-bounds. As we all know, slow play is the bane of most golfers' lives, particularly at weekends.

The third shot here at Monte Carlo, if the first two shots have been on target, will leave you about 75–95 yards to the pin. The very small green, with a narrow neck leading in between two bunkers, also slopes down towards the front: quite the opposite of the fairway which is downhill towards the green. The shot, therefore, needs to 'bite' as it lands. Charles demonstrated how to do it.

"First of all, set the base of the club aiming at the target" – in this case, being a fairly short shot, the flag itself – "and have the club shaft pointing directly at your belt buckle. Adopt a fairly wide stance to maintain good balance.

"Stand as upright as possible, keeping the back straight and bend from the knees, not the hips. During the backswing keep the feet firmly on the ground, pivoting from the hips up though

– on this distance you only need a half-swing. It is really vital to keep the back straight and upright.''

He pointed out the importance of keeping the left arm straight on the backswing, only cocking the wrists at the very last second.

Despite the restricted backswing, the follow-through needs to be fairly full and high. Distance will come automatically and the only thing to do is to swing smoothly through the ball. On short shots in particular the swing needs very careful timing. Practice will teach you just how slowly you can swing and still maintain control and obtain the right distance. The half-swing restricts the speed at impact but it is very important on this type of shot.

''Keep the club below the shoulders,'' Charles emphasized.

It feels a little strange at first but ten minutes in front of a mirror keeping the club below the shoulders, but the left arm straight, will make it feel comfortable.

The other uncomfortable feeling came from having the club totally upright. Many golfers have the club shaft pointing left, hands ahead of the ball. Charles recommends having the shaft upright. This allows you to put better loft on the ball, controlling it and stopping it faster on the green. It does also give you the opportunity of seeing that the club face – at the base – is pointing correctly. If the club is over the ball your view is restricted. This position allows you to see clearly and to align the club correctly.

That, and the backspin achieved, helps you control the ball on the approach shot to the green. That saves shots. And that is what it's all about!

The third shot to the very small green is less than 100-yards but needs careful control. The ball needs to 'bite' when it lands.

Sotogrande, Spain
Theodore Gonzalez, Club Professional

14th hole, 478 yards

The *Costa del Sol* in southern Spain is aptly named, for the sun does shine for well over 300 days a year. The coast has become home to thousands of refugees from northern European climes, eager to escape the cold, and plays host to millions of visitors. In recent years, too, golfers have started making a pilgrimage to this part of Spain for it offers some excellent golf courses: here the golf industry is growing faster than ever.

One of the best courses – many say *the* best – is at Sotogrande, not far east from Gibraltar, the huge and famous rock which was the landing point for the Moorish invasion of Spain in 786, when Al Tariq, the leader of the invaders, landed here, giving the place his name, Jabal Al Tar-iq.

The professional at Sotogrande is Theodore Gonzalez, who came here from Madrid in 1973. He took me out onto the 478-yard par-5 14th, a daunting hole which starts with a drive round the edge of a lake before heading uphill to a closely guarded green. Although beset with difficulties, including out-of-bounds left, the fairway, if you clear the lake, is wide, making the second and third shots look deceptively easy. Far from it!

That first shot from the tee is a real teaser – you can either play safe and aim left and very short, or, if your power and accuracy off the tee are good on that day you can aim long over

Theodore Gonzalez, from Madrid, is the Club Professional at Sotogrande on the Costa del Sol.

The dangerous temptation here is to try to cut off as much of the lake as possible. Aiming more to the left is safer but adds more distance to the second shot. This second shot should be pushed to the right.

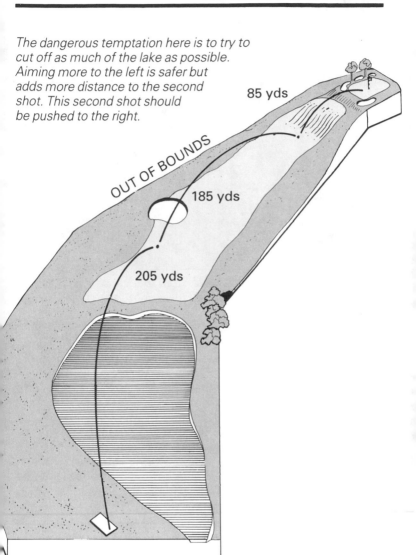

85 yds

OUT OF BOUNDS

185 yds

205 yds

Sotogrande

- **Try using fairway woods more frequently**
- **Don't treat a fairway wood like an iron but sweep through the ball**
- **Playing in wind test the strength and direction with each shot**
- **In high winds, keep the ball lower on approach shots**

The daunting view across the water from the tee, showing the dog-leg to the right on the far side. The shot from the tee is tricky.

the lake. From the tee, to clear the lake and land in the middle of the fairway, will require a shot of around 160 yards. A little further on is a huge bunker to the left, just waiting to catch the 'safe' shot.

Theodore's advice was to use the driver, and aim for the bunker, with a little fade.

"That should bring the ball far enough left not to play games with the water, but not too far left that you go out-of-bounds or end up in the rough," he suggested.

Another major factor here at Sotogrande is the wind, which not only gusts around, but changes direction a dozen times during the course of a round. That huge rock a few miles down the road acts as a funnel for winds hurtling in from the Atlantic, spinning round as they rush into the Mediterranean.

"Check the wind before every shot," Theodore advised. With the hole being a dog-leg, through the middle of the fairway at least, checking is vital.

The first shot did as it was told, leaving the ball sitting nicely in the left side of the fairway, on an area of springy grass.

"Fairway woods should be used more often," Theodore stated, showing me how to use a 3-wood off the grass for distance and accuracy.

"Grip very slightly down, just sufficiently to feel that you are controlling the club. Maintain the left arm as straight as possible on the backswing and don't go too far back on the backswing. The idea is to sweep the ball away, not dig at it as

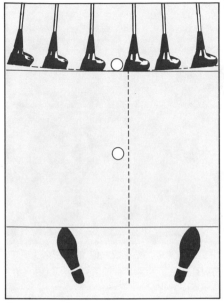 

(Above left) For a fairway wood the ball needs to be 'swept'
away, with the club connecting at the lowest point of the swing
arc. The ball is placed slightly forward.

(Above right) With an approach shot into the wind and uphill, the
ball has to be played well back in the stance, just in front of the
rear foot. The hands are pressed well forward.

you would for an iron.''

This is a common problem for average players – we try to
treat a fairway wood the same as an iron. The club head has to
sweep through the ball, pushing it away rather than hitting
down into it. For this reason the ball needs to be in the middle
of the stance, or very, very slightly forward.

The address position is vitally important, with the club sitting
squarely on the ground showing the correct loft of the club.
This is where you will strike the ball so it ought to be easier to
set up!

Theodore made me try the shot a few times before he was at
last satisfied.

''The club head has to spend as long as possible on the grass,
so keeping the arm straight will help get it down well. There
should be no divot, just a long 'scorch' mark on the grass.
Practise the shot without a ball until you can get that mark more
than one foot long.'' The follow-through needs to be aiming at
the hole, although not held back.

When the wind is strong it is advisable to check its force and direction before every shot. Here the trees and the flag are reliable indicators that the wind is whistling across the green.

That second shot gave a reasonable distance, just short of the uphill slope that leads to the green. He had told me to aim right, which I did. Getting close to the green it was obvious why, but unless you knew the course you might have stayed left – with potentially disastrous results.

The green itself is quite long, 45 yards from back to front with a very slight slope to the front, which is good for approach shots. However, the width can be a problem, so the closer in you get the second shot the better, but with the wind often against at this stage, it is rare to be able to threaten the green with the second shot. I managed a fair distance on that second shot, some 185 yards, leaving about 85 yards to the green.

At this point, to an elevated green, the wind was whistling across from the right, waiting to catch any high ball and knock it across to the bunkers which are between the trees (one tree is actually in the bunker) skirting the left of the green.

"Keep the ball low on the approach," Theodore told me. "Play it back in your stance, take a steeper swing path, as you might for a bunker shot, but not quite so exaggerated, and hit down on it with a less lofted club. That sends the ball to the green and keeps it there without going too high. Hitting down on it will give it sufficient backspin to stop it."

A couple of attempts did it – what an easy game this can seem when you take advice from someone as good as this – and then practise!

The Australian GC, Sydney, Australia

Ron Luxton, Club Professional

18th hole, 520 yards

This is the course that Jack built. Jack Nicklaus, that is, and it was in 1975 that he redesigned it and supervised its construction, paid for by Kerry Packer, one of the club's members and a familiar name to cricket-followers.

The club itself was founded in 1882 when golf was played at nearby Moore Park, today a well-maintained municipal course just up the road. The Australian moved to its present location in 1903, but a series of course alterations and reconstruction has continued up to today.

The maintenance of the course and facilities is just one of the reasons why so many top tournaments, including the Australian Open, are held here.

The club's professional is Ron Luxton, widely acknowledged as one of Australia's foremost teachers. He chose for our lesson the closing hole on the course, the 475-metre (520 yard) par-5 18th, a long hole where water comes into play on the second and third shots.

"From the tee the first shot is fairly straightforward," he told me. "The bunker comes into play at 207 metres (227 yards) so

Ron Luxton, Club Professional at The Australian GC, Sydney, one of Australia's finest courses.

71

The approach shot has to take into account the water on the right.

only the longest hitters will have to contend with it.

"The average player will just need to aim very slightly to left of that bunker and hit straight or with slight draw. A slice or fade is no good here: the ball needs to kick left."

For a player who can reach close to 200 metres (220 yards) the second shot leaves him with something like 170 metres (185 yards) to the start of the water on the right, so a careful shot is needed.

Having hit just four metres short of the bunker – the draw and roll bringing the ball to the centre of the fairway as well as

Australian GC, Sydney

- Play steady, careful golf. No big-hitting. No trick shots
- On hard ground, play the ball at the lowest point of the swing arc
- Practise accuracy
- Check your grip regularly

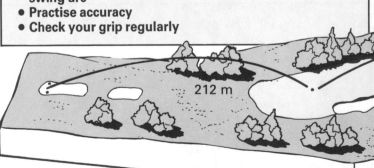

212 m

The tee-shot should present no problem, but a good second, placed left, will definitely pay dividends, avoiding the water on the right of the green. The approach must not be left short.

The green is fairly tricky, with a dangerous side on the right.

giving it a few extra metres – I was left with 168 metres (184 yards) to the edge of the water.

Despite the hole's appearance on the plan of the course, the best approach is from the right of the fairway, closer to the water. This is primarily because of the roll of the fairway.

"Try, however, not to go too far right off the fairway," Ron emphasized to me.

"In the rough it's easy to get a 'flier' – a ball that, because grass gets between it and the clubface, reduces its backspin, rather like having less grip with a bald tyre.

"With less backspin the ball comes out lower and flies further, bouncing on when it hits the green rather than pulling up. I would suggest, if you are faced with such a shot, that you might consider using one club less, a 8 rather than an 7.

"Here, though, you have the lake to contend with, so you

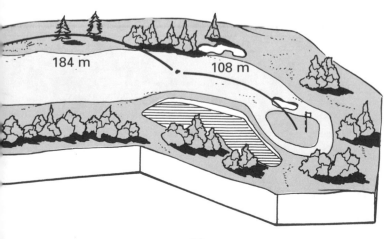

shouldn't take risks. Use a club with which you can comfortably reach the green.''

Fortunately my shot had not strayed off so a 9-iron the 99 metres (108 yards) to the pin did the job, leaving two putts for a par.

It was achieved by following Ron's advice and just playing careful, steady golf. No big-hitting, no trick shots.

''What about playing on patches of hard ground?'' I queried.

''You have to play the ball at the lowest point of the swing arc. Normally you play the ball as the club is still coming down (except off the tee when you are playing it with the club going up). But off hard ground get it right at the lowest point, almost lifting it off clean. The ball needs to be a little further forward, about three inches inside the left heel.

''If you find, off hard ground, that you're pulling the ball left, try having the ball a little further forward.

''Having the ball forward will, of course, gain you extra height, making the ball more controllable as it lands, but it will cost you a little in distance, so be prepared to take one club more. Yet you need to remember that in hot, dry weather the ball flies further anyway – but not in very high humidity.''

''Far too many players,'' he told me, ''*try to play beyond their capabilities*. Particularly when they're in trouble, they try shots that even I wouldn't consider practical. If they would just stick to what they know they would have lower scores. Be more conservative. Don't try to over-hit. Play it gently and don't

A look back from the green shows just how far the water comes into play on the fourteenth.

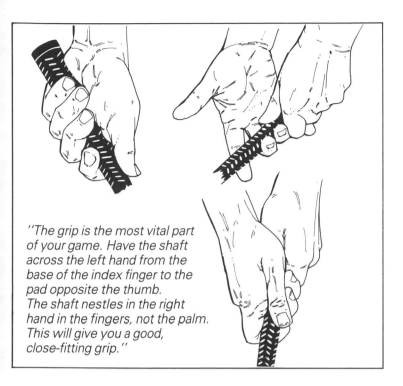

"The grip is the most vital part of your game. Have the shaft across the left hand from the base of the index finger to the pad opposite the thumb.
The shaft nestles in the right hand in the fingers, not the palm. This will give you a good, close-fitting grip."

expect quite so much from each shot. Practise *accuracy* rather than just uncontrolled power."

He explained that most golfers fail to grip the club correctly and thus cannot play the game to their full potential.

"The grip is the most vital part of golf yet to most people it's boring. Taking one minute to learn the correct grip will save you hours of work on your swing. Here's what to do.

"Take the club in your left hand. Have the shaft across the palm from the first joint of the index finger to the fleshy part of the palm opposite the thumb. The thumb then comes down on the front of the shaft.

"The right-hand grip has the clubshaft across the first joint of the fingers, *not* in the palm. The fingers close on the shaft, over the left thumb and with the little finger overlapping the index finger of the left hand.

"As you swing back, the left thumb, straight down the shaft, will be supporting the club and will help you begin pulling down on the club with the left hand, rather than having the right hand pushing.

"Thus you get power and control. And that is exactly what you want!"

Frankfurt, West Germany
Henning Strüver, Club Professional

17th hole, 472 yards

Hidden away in woods, a few kilometres from the edge of the runway at Frankfurt Airport, is the beautiful Frankfurter Golf Club, home for several years to the German Open. The club was founded in 1913 and is housed in an imposing country mansion. Not a pitch away from the first tee is the Pro Shop, run by the genial Henning Strüver, who has been at Frankfurt since 1965, before which he spent a couple of years as a player on the European Tour.

Over the years he has steadily built up a reputation as a good teacher and nowadays is much in demand for his skills, both at his own club and throughout Germany.

The Frankfurt course has three par-5 holes, each of them very different in character. We chose the 472-yard 17th, a left-hand dog-leg with the tee shot being a difficult, uphill, blind shot. The distance is from the normal men's tee, the players in the German Open having to play an extra fifteen yards back.

The drive, uphill, with the land sloping very steeply from right to left towards a large bunker 190 yards off the tee, is over

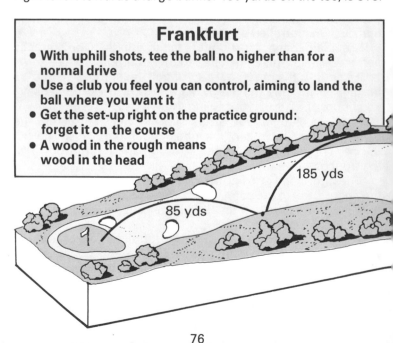

Frankfurt

- **With uphill shots, tee the ball no higher than for a normal drive**
- **Use a club you feel you can control, aiming to land the ball where you want it**
- **Get the set-up right on the practice ground: forget it on the course**
- **A wood in the rough means wood in the head**

185 yds

85 yds

Henning Strüver, Frankfurt's top professional.

rough, so the drive needs height as well as distance.

"The aim is to get the tee-shot past the bunker onto the fairway," explained Henning. "With an uphill shot the ball needs teeing no higher than you would for a normal drive," he continued, changing my opinion on how to get the ball higher by teeing it higher.

"That cuts down distance," he explained. "But don't use a driver. Take a 3-wood, or a 2- or 3-iron. Even a 4-iron, if you connect squarely, will reach the fairway and be far more controllable than the driver. Aim to land the ball where you want it and thus use a club you feel you can control."

A habit of mine, when using an iron off the tee, was to tee the ball lower than for a wood. I think this came about from watching the pros on television, who seem to sink the tee

The tee-shot needs to be long and slightly right; the second a little left (though I went too far!).

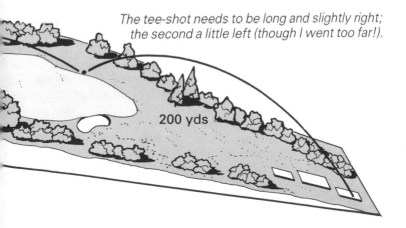

200 yds

The view from the tee, showing why you must stay right, avoiding the bunker and slope.

almost totally into the ground for iron shots. Henning changed this habit and it was to prove successful.

I asked about the set-up.

"Get it right on the practice ground and forget it!" he responded. "On the tee just get the body aligned correctly and the club face square to the target. Forget all this going through a dozen points as you begin the backswing. Too many golfers try to remember to get the left arm straight, keep the head still, turn the shoulders, kick in with the left knee and so on. All they should really be concentrating on is hitting the ball to a predetermined target.

"All the other factors in the swing must be practised elsewhere and should be automatic. When you get to the tee just concentrate on hitting the ball in the right direction, otherwise you become like an airline captain going through a checklist before take-off."

I used a 2-iron and did exactly what he told me, aiming slightly right of the bunker. The ball flew up well, not so high that it lost much distance, and fading slightly just before it landed, showing that I had hit the ball with the club face slightly open at the point of impact.

The ball cleared the bunker safely enough though. When we reached it, it was sitting up in some very light rough.

"I often see players trying to hit a wood out of the rough," Henning told me. "I always say that *wood in the rough means wood in the head*.

"If the ball is in thick rough use a 7-iron or upwards to dig it out with a gentle but firm swing and a full, high follow-through. If you are in trouble just get the ball back out onto the fairway with whatever distance you can manage. Never be tempted to try a 'career-best' shot – it won't work!"

From where my ball lay to the green was about 270 yards, with a bunker sitting threateningly on the right about 100 yards from the flag. I hit a 5-iron, 'swishing' it through the grass, almost lifting the ball from the grass. With my inherent handicapper's habit of imagining I would overhit it, the ball stayed short and, with the effect of the grass closing the club face (it does it every time so you should open the face a little), turned slightly left.

The ball was sitting on parched, cracked, bare earth as hard as concrete. Earlier in the summer, a very hot, dry one, I had had great problems playing off patches of ground like this, the club bouncing off the ground, 'shanking' right on almost every occasion. I asked Henning how to cure this.

"Have the ball well back in your stance with the weight mainly on your left leg, take a half-swing and feel that you are dragging the ball foward."

The first time I tried this, using an 8-iron with about 85 yards to go, I 'chopped' at the ball, not following through. As there was no-one following behind I had another attempt, this time extending the follow-through about the same length as the backswing, like a pendulum. It felt much smoother and the ball landed on the front of the green, clearing two bunkers on the way. It did not spin back but pulled up fairly quickly, leaving me a 10-yard putt – which I missed but cleaned up second time. Ignoring the first 'hashed' shot off the bare ground, I had scored a five. With the stroke index of six, I had gained a net 'birdie' – without hitting the ball hard or great distances, the shots travelling 195 yards, 185 and 85 yards – and had been off the fairway on the first two shots. So by thinking of where you want the ball to go, and how you want to hit it, it is easier to pick up a net birdie.

As we left the course, Henning repeated his advice: "Play simple, controlled shots rather than trying to get great distance. Play down the middle, using a 5-iron all the way if you like. You might not cut many strokes off the card but you will definitely stop wasting shots.

"Keep it simple. Play the shots you know you can play – not those you would like to play!"

Boca Raton, Florida, USA
Ron Polane, Director of Golf

9th hole, 563 yards

"Most club golfers, when faced with playing into the wind, tend to try to over-hit the ball, thinking that, in order to have it travel a sufficient distance into a stiff breeze, they have to swing faster and need to hit harder.

"They're wrong!"

The words of wisdom come from Ron Polane, Director of Golf at the beautiful Boca Raton Country Club on Florida's Atlantic coast. Ron has been at Boca since 1963 when he joined the legendary Sam Snead as assistant pro. He had in fact grown up in the shadow of the great man, at Hot Springs, Virginia, where his father ran a hotel. When Sam retired in 1969 Ron took over the top position at Boca and now runs regular golf clinics, aided by four assistant pros.

The course was re-laid in 1988 so plays differently than when Sam Snead was playing it not too many years back, and from when Tomy Armour was the club pro between 1926 and 1955.

The hole that Ron chose for his lesson was the 563 yard par-5 ninth (598 yards from the back tee).

The tee shot on the 565-yard par-5 is normally played into a

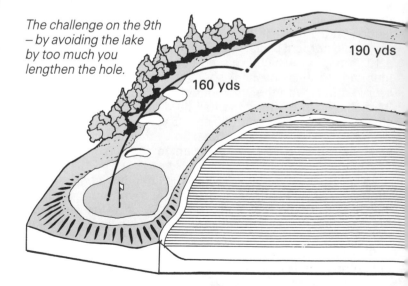

The challenge on the 9th – by avoiding the lake by too much you lengthen the hole.

190 yds

160 yds

Looking towards the green on the 9th at Boca Raton

stiff cross-breeze from left to right and slightly against. The perfect tee shot would be to drive the ball to the left side of the fairway, letting the breeze move the ball back into the centre. In windy conditions remember to swing within yourself. A solid hit is much less affected by wind than a forced, miss-hit shot.

A well struck, but not over-struck, 1-iron or perhaps a 3-

Boca Raton

- Don't try to overhit the ball in windy conditions but let the club do the work
- Test the wind by throwing a blade of grass and look carefully at the trees around you
- With approach shots into the wind go for the back of the green; most club golfers land short

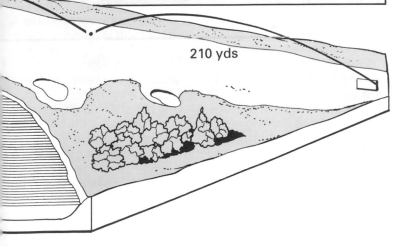

210 yds

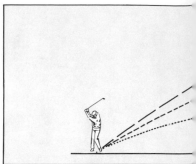

(Above) A flat approach shot will run up; most people hit short. "Take more club and you'll reach the pin," says Ron Polane.

(Left) To hit a low shot keep the ball back in your stance, hands well ahead.

wood, aiming almost at the right-most trap, with the stance a little open to get the fade will put the ball in the middle of the fairway. It should carry about 150–180 yards depending on how well you connect.

The traps are between 170 and 235 yards from the back tee so this first shot ought to be landing almost abreast of them.

The second shot presents a problem. The entrance to the green is very narrow, being protected on the left by a lake; and on the right by more sand traps. The distance now to the green is over 350 yards, so a well-struck 4-iron, or a fairway wood if you're comfortable with one, should lay the ball up close to the 150 yard marker.

I went for the 4-iron, a club I personally hit straighter than a 3-wood off the fairway. This far out from the green the wind is still blowing but as the hole is dog-legged the wind is more directly in front. A low shot, therefore, with the ball slightly further back in the stance, is the one to hit. The effect of having the ball back in the stance is to straighten up the club face and this keeps it low. With less loft and backspin the ball will bounce on and on if the fairway is hard.

Having stayed slightly right, if anything, to keep away from the dreaded lake, the third shot should present nothing more than a 6- or 7-iron pitch onto the green, going now for a high shot to land accurately on the middle of the green.

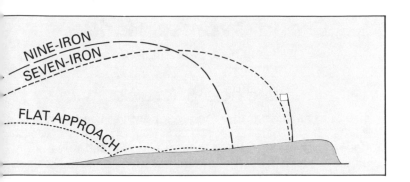

"The average player will be short," warned Ron, "because the green slopes towards the front. The wind is always blowing, too, though the green is protected so the wind appears not to be there." A look at the flag confirmed that the green itself was protected from the wind by the historic hotel building, though the approach shot into the green will, with a ball hit high, be held back. It *is* difficult to judge wind exactly but consider the example of Curtis Strange. He tests the strength and direction before every shot by throwing a blade of grass into the wind. He then looks carefully at trees around him on the direction of the shot.

"Take an extra club and forget the flag – just go for the back of the green and be careful not to hit it over the green completely. Most golfers land short – they seem to have an inherent fear of going past the flag and tend to hit their approach shots flat. They will bounce and roll on, of course, particularly on the faster greens in America. If, on those approach shots they were to put more height on the ball by hitting under it more, the ball would lift better and sit down faster once it hit the green. Once they have practised it on the range they would understand that they can aim directly at the flag, particularly into the wind. The average golfer will not be able to generate the degree of back-spin which pro golfers can. That comes from perfect timing and the height of the ball. The average club golfer should forget it and aim for the flag, with an extra club and greater height. If he connects cleanly – which is an art that comes from practice – he will be able to land the ball softly, very close to the pin."

The green is huge – some 160 feet from back to front – and there is no danger behind it, even though the clubhouse appears to be right behind the green.

Hitting a 6- or even 5-iron to the middle of the green should give you two putts for a 'birdie' five, or par if you happen to have a low handicap.

Grand Cypress, Florida
Paul Celano, Director of Golf

2nd hole, 513 yards

It seems to have been there much longer yet Grand Cypress, with its three courses in the shadow of Disney's Magic Kingdom and Epcot Center, just outside Orlando, was only opened in 1984. The New Course, designed by Jack Nicklaus and modelled on St Andrews, opened in 1988. The New Course is a full eighteen holes; the North, South and East are nines.

The second hole on the South course is a test of accuracy and of a golfer's temperament. A lake runs along the entire length of this 513-yard par-5 dog-leg right, before cutting across in front of the green.

From the tee accuracy is important yet the big hitter will gain a premium, as the further forward he can take his second shot the easier it becomes to place it in the perfect position to hit the green on the third one.

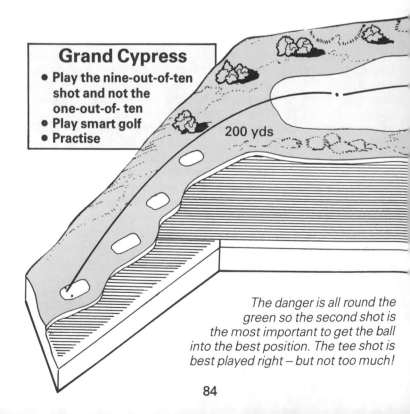

Grand Cypress
- **Play the nine-out-of-ten shot and not the one-out-of- ten**
- **Play smart golf**
- **Practise**

200 yds

The danger is all round the green so the second shot is the most important to get the ball into the best position. The tee shot is best played right – but not too much!

84

"Practise! Practise! Practise!"

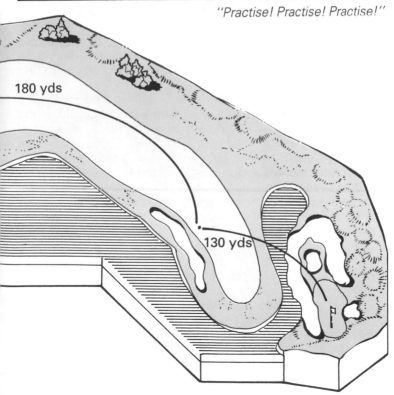

180 yds

130 yds

Jack Nicklaus, Steve Pate and Ian Baker-Finch are regulars at the imposing Grand Cypress Club.

"The lake on the right should not really be a factor, particularly off the tee," said Paul Celano, the Director of Golf at Grand Cypress.

"There is plenty of room on the left with fairly large mounds to protect the ball should you veer too far left. With the average player tending to slice, the best shot is towards those mounds but as far right as you feel confident of hitting. The driver is the best club because distance off the tee pays off later and there is a fairly wide area to hit at."

Only the first 120 yards off the tee – unless the slice is very bad – involve the water, but any golfer who is nervous of the lake can play safe by aiming left to go round. A tee shot of around 200 yards is perfect here, particularly if you can bring it round right, leaving some 280 yards to run. The blue tee is 513 yards, resort tee 478 and Ladies' 445, and for any mathematicians the measurements are taken down the centre of the fairway. So cutting corners cuts distance, as long as you stay out of trouble – the further right, the shorter will be the remaining distance.

The second shot will vary depending on that tee shot. A short tee shot, landing left, will have further to go, so it is best to hit long on the second shot, aiming for the middle of the fairway or very slightly right, but taking into account that lake.

"For the well placed, long tee shot, the second shot becomes much simpler," Paul explained. "The best approach to the green is from the right corner of the fairway, so the second shot should be aiming to lay up just before the lake."

Such a shot would mean a distance of around 170–180 yards – reachable with a 4-iron, or perhaps a fairway wood if you have a good lie. From there the good player will be able to pitch across onto the green in regulation and take two putts for a five.

The player further back and left has to hit well to get close to the green but on his third shot can do one of two things.

"He can either lay up right, as did the second shot of the better player, or, if he feels confident, he can carry the water guarding the green. The pin position and the shape of the green make it difficult to hit, so the average-handicap player should lay up and take his six for par."

Play safe is the motto for anyone in doubt. The hole has an index of eight so that extra shot is useful to those who need it. The green is also surrounded by sand traps so accuracy here is extremely important.

"This is where the high-handicap player can really score," said Paul. "By planning his shots and playing the percentage shots—playing safe if you will—he can pick up shots here really quite easily.

"Don't gamble unnecessarily. Play the nine-out-of-ten shot, not the one-out-of-ten!"

Playing safe here and practising those short chips and pitches rather than trying to hit a ball 300 yards down the fairway, will pay off.

"Play smart golf," Paul emphasised, "and practise."

Certainly practising at Grand Cypress would put you in good company, for several of the Tour members, including Greg Norman (the Resident Touring Pro), Nick Price, Ian Baker-Finch and Steve Pate are among twenty-five of the US Tour pros who improve their technique here.

The green! Water, sand and a tiny area to aim at. Strong nerves and a steady hand are needed here.

Wentworth, Surrey, UK

17th hole, 571 yards

At Wentworth, one of the most famous golf clubs in the world, I reached the end of my lessons on how to play par-5s. My teachers had given me a great deal to work on and it was time to test the results.

All I had learnt was now, hopefully, going to come back into my mind at the right time. *Take the wind into account. Think like a chess player to plan the shots you most want. Do not over-hit but play within your capabilities. Look for the direction in which the fairway slopes. Have a definite target to aim at, even though it may be out of reach.* All these thoughts and more came back rather like the night-before-the-exam revision.

Choosing the right hole on which to test all this theory was another problem, but it was solved by Richard Doyle-Davidson, Wentworth's Managing Director.

"The long 17th here on the West Course," Richard told me,

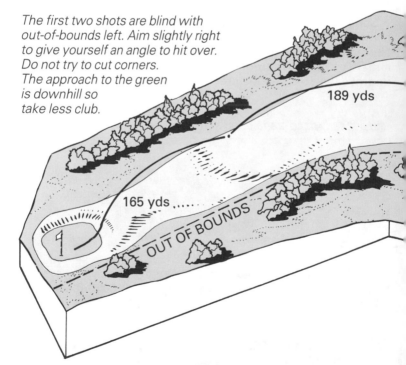

The first two shots are blind with out-of-bounds left. Aim slightly right to give yourself an angle to hit over. Do not try to cut corners. The approach to the green is downhill so take less club.

189 yds

165 yds

OUT OF BOUNDS

I have managed to stay right, giving an angle at which to aim.

"has to be one of the most difficult in golf to get home in two. Even the top professionals have to hit perfect shots to reach the green in two to set up a birdie. Few of them achieve it. Amateur players find it impossible to reach the green in two from the

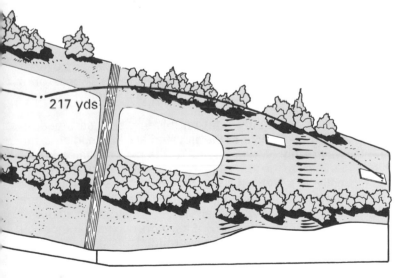

217 yds

championship tee, and have to hit three excellent shots to reach the green.

"The first two shots are completely blind because you only see the green as you come over the hill 165 yards out.

"There is also out-of-bounds the whole way down the left of

Choosing the correct spot for the tee-shot is vital. Here I have chosen a 3-wood for accuracy as the aiming point is not very wide. I need to go slightly right.

the hole, which curves sharply left. The right is protected by trees and the fairway slopes to the right, pushing the ball out. Go too far left and, if you stay on the fairway, you have nothing to work with on the next shot.''

As I teed up I remembered the advice of Henning Strüver of Frankfurt and Gregor Jamieson at Lake None: ''Focus on a specific target''. This was not the time to be worrying about grip, or swing-plane.

I wanted to go slightly right on this first shot so I teed up pretty well in the middle of the elevated tee, the road crossing the fairway being 203 yards out. To the road the fairway just slopes away from the tee, with only a slight slope to the right.

I normally hit a 3-wood 200 yards off the tee, with some roll. Today that roll would be minimal but with an elevated tee there should be a few extra yards' carry. I remembered the advice of George Will at Royal Waterloo: ''First work out the distance you can comfortably achieve. Don't over-hit''.

The driver gains a few extra yards but often loses direction for most of us middle and higher handicappers. Using the 3-wood off the tee enables us to hit straighter shots to where we want them, rather than spraying them into the trees.

Smoke from a bonfire in the garden of one of the large properties lining the course was starting to make my tee shot a little more difficult. I recalled the advice from Liam Higgins at

Waterville: "Don't stand over the ball thinking of birdies and pars. Just get on with your game".

Aiming very slightly right I hit a 3-wood well, giving it some extra height to use what wind there was behind me. The ball bounced just before the road, carried it and landed 217 yards out from the tee, in almost the perfect position, though the route to the green was still blind.

Three hundred and fifty four yards to go. The route left cut off by that out-of-bounds, as Mr Doyle-Davidson reminded me. Most of my teachers would have suggested that a fairway wood is the best choice here, as the shot needs to be fairly straight and as long as possible without straining.

Another 3-wood? Perhaps, or if you are confident using one, a long iron. My preference is for a 2-iron.

I lined up the 2-iron, aiming just left of a grassy mound. Keeping my body square to the target, the ball about three inches inside the left heel, arms free and stretching very slightly for the ball but not so as to lose balance, the right shoulder coming back on the take-away but with the wrists held firm, I swung smoothly and made good solid contact.

The ball went straight where I had aimed it, landing just left of the mound. The shot measured 189 yards. Just 165 yards to go!

The third shot is the first time that you can see the green. From this distance I would normally hit a 5-iron, but the approach to the green is downhill with no bunkers and hardly any wind, so a 6-iron was my choice.

*The 6-iron landed very slightly left leaving me this putt for a birdie.
I knocked it a foot past the pin.*

For a distance of 165 yards which club would you choose? I
know that I normally hit a 5-iron 165 yards. Should I reach for
the 5-iron, then? Theory would say, yes. But I thought carefully.
The approach to the green was obviously downhill as I could
see the top of the flag but not the green itself. With a slope
down to the green and no hazards at all to worry about, a
5-iron might be too much.

I took the 6-iron, aiming for the safe, left side of the green,
knowing that, without straining, I could hit the green. And I did.

With two well-placed and well-hit shots and one 'easy' 6-
iron, I, a 14-handicapper, was on the green of one of the longest
par-5s in the world! Two putts and the ball ended up where it
should, giving me a gross five, a score with which many
professionals would be happy. Furthermore, with my handicap
and the stroke index of 8, I picked up a stroke and ended with a
net birdie.

So, how would you do on a par-5 after learning from the
professionals in this book? Try it, go out and play the hardest
par-5 on your home course. Don't play it like you always play it
– think about it, use the professionals' advice and ideas and see
if you can achieve a net par or better on a regular basis. But stay
relaxed and don't try to hit shots with which you are not happy.
Playing to our own capabilities is very important in golf.

Glossary of Golfing Terms

Ace A hole in one.

Address The position taken by a player in relation to his ball when ready to play a stroke.

Approach A shot played to the green. An approach putt is played from long distance when the player does not expect to hole out.

Arc The path of the clubhead during a golf swing.

As it lies A player is obliged to play his ball from the position it has come to rest after his previous shot unless otherwise specified by the rules of golf or local rules.

Backspin Rotation of a golf ball which causes it to fly high, grip the turf when it strikes the ground and sometimes to spin back towards the player.

Backswing The total movement of body and club away from the ball until the swing becomes a movement back towards it.

Ball moved A ball is said to have moved if it does not return to its original position once it has been at rest. This is usually caused by a player grounding his club behind the ball or removing loose impediments near it. In either case, there is a one stroke penalty.

Blade To strike the ball with the bottom edge of the club. The result is usually a thinned or topped shot, but can be deliberate.

Bogey A score of one over par on a hole. Traditional British golfers use it in its original sense of the score on a hole that a competent golfer who is not a long hitter ought to make.

Borrow To aim off in putting to allow for sideslopes to bring the ball back to the hole.

Boundary The perimeter of a course. To go beyond these limits is to be out-of-bounds and suffer the stroke and distance penalty.

Bunker A depression, either deep or shallow on the course, usually part filled with sand and either natural or man-made. Earth and grass bunkers can also be found.

Carry The distance from where the ball is played to where it lands. Often used when there is an obstacle to be carried, such as a water hazard, a fairway bunker or a ravine.

Casual water Temporary water on the course which is not part of the design and is therefore not a water hazard. The player is allowed to pick and drop without penalty. If water is brought to the surface when the player takes his stance he can also claim relief from casual water. Snow and ice may be treated either as casual water or as loose impediments.

Championship tees Some courses have teeing areas farther back than the medal tees for championship and tournament use only.

Chip A low running shot played from close to the green towards the flag.

Choke down To grip lower on the club when either less length or more control are needed.

Closed face To address the ball or strike it with the toe of the club turned inwards.

Closed stance Used when a right-handed player has his left foot nearer to the target line than the right.

Clubhead That part of the club which is fixed to a shaft and is used to strike the ball.

Cocking the wrists The bend or break in the wrists as the club is swung back from the ball.

Come off the shot This is said of a player whose body lifts up before his clubhead contacts the ball or whose shoulders turn away too early. There can be several results which include a topped shot, a quick hook or a slice, depending on the timing.

Dead A ball is dead when it is so close to the hole that it seems impossible to miss the putt.

Divot A piece of turf removed from the ground by the clubhead in the playing of a shot.

Dog-leg A hole where the fairway bends sharply left or right at driving distance. There is often a hazard, such as a bunker, bushes or rough at the angle of the dog-leg to discourage players from attempting to drive across it.

Dormy A player in matchplay is dormy when he has moved as many holes up as there remain to be played. He cannot be beaten unless the match goes to extra holes.

Downhill lie When the player has to strike his ball from a downslope.

Draw A gentle movement of the ball from right to left in the case of a right-handed player.

Drive A full shot played from the tee, usually but not necessarily with a driver.

Drop A player drops a ball when he has hit out-of-bounds or lost his original ball. He may also drop his ball back into play when given relief by the rules or under penalty if he thinks the ball unplayable.

Eagle A score of two under par on a hole.

Etiquette The conduct expected of players towards opponents, other golfers on the course and the course itself.

Extension A term used of the stretching of the arms through and after impact and usually considered essential in a good swing.

Face The part of the clubhead intended to strike the ball. Also the part of the bunker that confronts the player as he makes his shot. The term is not used unless the face is steep or rises some distance from the floor of the bunker.

Fade A shot which flies straight for much of its flight and then, in the case of a right-handed player, drifts from left to right.

Fairway The closely mown part of a golf hole between the tee and the green. Its boundaries will usually be semi-rough or rough and the apron of the green.

Flat swing A backswing where the club is swung back nearer the horizontal than vertical so that the club passes over the top of the upper arm or the lower. In spite of the example of Ben Hogan, this came to be considered a fault with the successes of Jack Nicklaus. The pendulum is now swinging the other way.

Flyer A shot, usually into the green, where the ball flies further than the player intended. It is usually caused by grass, especially if wet, coming between clubface and ball with reduction of backspin.

Follow through The movement of the body, especially the arms, after the ball has been struck.

Forward tees Set ahead of the medal tees, these are mainly used either to make the course slightly easier for general play or to reduce wear on the competition teeing area.

Fourball Usually a match in which two count their better ball score against the better ball of the other two players.

Foursome A match for four players, with each pair using one ball and hitting alternate shots on each hole. Before play begins the team of two decided who is to hit the first tee shot. The other will then play from the second tee, and so on.

Free drop A drop without penalty, such as away from ground under repair or casual water.

Gimme A putt short enough to be conceded.

Go down the shaft To grip lower to improve control of the club, or sometimes to reduce the distance obtained from a particular club.

Grain Grass on a green where the blades are not vertical but lie horizontal in some direction. This is sometimes natural but usually caused by cutting. A putt with the grain travels further than one against it.

Heel The part of the clubhead nearest the golfer as he prepares to play. Also where the shaft enters.

Hitting across The movement of the clubhead from out to in at impact, and one cause of a slice.

Hole This must be four and a quarter inches in diameter and sunk to a depth of four inches. The liner must be set one inch or more below the surface. The word is also applied to the entire area between tee and green.

Hood To set the hands ahead of the clubface and therefore to reduce the loft of the club.

Hook A poor shot which curves from right to left in an exaggerated way, usually unintentionally.

Hosel The part of iron clubhead into which the shaft is fitted.

Identify A player must always be able to identify his ball. The brand name and a number are not sufficient and a personal mark should be added.

Interlocking grip A grip where the hands are bonded together by wrapping forefinger and little finger round each other.

Ladies' tees The par of golf courses and individual holes is rated differently for women than men. Ladies' tees are normally set ahead of those for men but may occasionally be set farther back, perhaps to make a par four into a five.

Let through When one game on a course waves another through, usually because of slower play or a lost ball.

Lie The position of the ball in relation to the ground beneath. A good lie usually means that most of the ball is visible. A lie becomes progressively worse as the ball settles down in the grass or sand. The term is also used of the way a clubhead sits on the turf. This depends on the angle formed by the clubhead with the shaft and whether or not the player stands near or far from the ball or if he holds his hands high or low. Players often have the lie of their iron clubs checked if they think one of more is either too upright or flat.

Lift and drop The action of a player when, under penalty or not, he picks up his ball and drops it in a place and manner laid down in the rules of golf.

Local rules Rules made by a club committee to deal with special conditions on the course.

Loft The angle a clubface is set back from the vertical. Among the irons, the loft increases from the No. one to the sand wedge.

Matchplay The form of golf based on holes won, lost and halved rather than total strokes taken.

Medal Originally these were competitions, usually strokeplay but occasionally matchplay, where a medal was the prize, held for a year or perhaps for ever.

Medal play Strokeplay competitions, with the lowest score winning.

Medal tees The competitions tees at a golf club at the distance the hole was designed to be played from.

Members' tees Tees set a few or more yards ahead of the medal tees for friendly play by members.

Mixed foursome Normal foursomes play except a woman is paired with a man.

Mulligan A second chance given to a golfer who has hit a poor first drive. This is against the rules of golf. It is allowed only in the friendliest of games and even then usually only on the first tee.

Municipal course A course owned by a public body rather than a private club and usually open to all.

Nap A term which refers to the horizontal growth of grass on a putting green, especially in South Africa. A ball putted against the nap will go less far than one hit with the same strength with the slope of the grass. Putting across the nap can be more puzzling.

Neck Part of the clubhead where the shaft is inserted.

Never up, never in A putt which does not reach the hole, and cannot possibly hole out.

Nineteenth When the first hole is played again after a match has finished all-square after 18 holes, it is referred as 'the 19th'. Also referred to as the bar in the clubhouse after a match, the 19th hole.

Open stance To stand to the ball with the front foot drawn back from the target line.

Out The first nine holes. The use derives from many early links courses where the players went 'out' for nine holes and the second nine took them 'in' to the clubhouse.

Out to in A swing path where the clubhead comes from outside the line of flight and moves inside at impact. If, at this time, the clubface is square or open, a slice results; if shut, the ball will be pulled.

Par The standard score for a hole, in most countries based on its lengfth. Holes up to 250 yards are par threes; up to 475 yards par fours and over 478 yards the remainder par fives.

Penalty stroke A stroke or strokes added to a score because of a breach of the rules of golf.

Pin high A shot to the green which finishes level with the flagstick but not necessarily close to it.

Pitch A fairly high shot played to a green from approximately 150 yards down to shots of just a few yards. The eight, nine wedge and sand iron are usually regarded as the pitching clubs.

Pitch and run A shot of lower trajectory than the pitch usually intended to land short of a green and run on to the flag. Not often played when greens are well watered.

Punch shot A shot played mainly with the forearms, with the hands in front of the clubhead and with the wrists held firm.

Push A shot which flies right of target and straight, caused by the swing path being to the right of the target.

Rough Grass which has been allowed to grow in order to penalize off-line shots.

Sand iron A usually heavy club with a flange designed so that the clubhead rises through soft sand rather than digs down. The rear of the flange, not the leading edge of the club, is lower.

Semi-rough The grass between the fairway and the uncut rough. Considerable attention is often paid to its length and density in important events.

Shank To hit a ball, using an iron at the place where the head joins the shaft. The ball flies away from the player nearly at right angles.

Stance The placing of the feet before playing a shot.

Stroke index For the purpose of giving and receiving strokes, all club cards are rated from one to 18 because it is reckoned a good player can be expected to play the most difficult holes more effectively than the poor player. In practice, however, strokes are equally divided between the first and second nines of the 18 holes so the system depends on deciding which is the most difficult hole on the course and the second most difficult is then reckoned to be in the other nine. So the numbering continues, alternating.

Trajectory The flight of a golf ball and the characteristics of its parabola.

Yardage charts Printed or personally prepared charts of golf holes which show the distances from one point on a hole to another.

Yips Caused by nerves when putting, this distressing condition can make a player unable to swing his putter back and his eventual stroke becomes a convulsive jerk or a jab. Self-confidence is lost.